THE
BOSTON
HUSTLE

THE BOSTON HUSTLE

the
hairspray,
the
cologne,
the
disco
and the
betrayal

JOEY CARVELLO
CHRISTOPHER R. MOORE

EDITED BY KIM COSTA

PALMETTO
P U B L I S H I N G
Charleston, SC
www.PalmettoPublishing.com

Hardcover ISBN: 979-8-8229-4575-3
Paperback ISBN:979-8-8229-3616-4
eBook ISBN: 979-8-8229-3617-1

Executive Producers:
Mark Finkelstein & Ellen Carvello

Independent Publishing Consultant: David Jurman

Cover Design by www.bcdbooks.com

Cover photo by Richard Maciejko

TABLE OF CONTENTS

FOREWORD

Boston today is a far cry from the town it was in the early years of our lives. It was a wonderful place and time to grow up, and yet that may have been because those of us who were young, full of new ideas, and enthusiastic for life didn't really comprehend the socioeconomic and racial tensions that surrounded us yet. We kept to ourselves and stuck with our crews, our neighbors, our friends, and our ways.

Boston was just Boston to us. Mention the word "Feast" and people would immediately picture the dollars pinned to a photo of the Blessed Mother being lowered from the third floor of a tenement window tethered to a string of yarn. Swinging in the breeze, it would come to rest in the outstretched hands of the faithful eager to capture it and attach it to the embroidered robe surrounding the statue, a statue which sat firmly on the shoulders of four massive men who took their job seriously. By the time they got through the neighborhood, there might have been as much as thirty thousand dollars attached to pictures pinned to her robe. You could never forget that sight. Or someone might even recall the old music they would play at those feasts, often out of tune with sloppy timing, but make no mistake, and despite the music, the throngs of people were alive: loving, laughing, eating. That was the way the world was. The rub only came later when we realized that all those people looked just like us.

I remember we weren't particularly concerned with black and white relations as kids, though the topic was always there in conversations we overheard our parents have or with the older kids who used to make racial slurs in an overly animated way that made us think that it was an important issue for us too. I guess it was a manner of soft indoctrination, albeit not one that was drummed into our heads or expected that we should practice. Nevertheless, it was there, and aside from the slurs there was a segregation of sorts that at times could cause some high-anxiety moments. We had areas of the city where each nationality and ethnicity congregated and kept to their own, as if distinct lines had been embedded in the invisible boundaries at the edges of town. And as we grew and ventured out of our neighborhoods, we could easily find ourselves out of the comfort zone of home turf.

But the one thing that did seem to break the stress and allowed each of the opposing factions to find common ground and exhale, if only for a few hours a week, was the music—when we finally found it. That wonderful, happy, positive message of Disco music, and the tingling sensation and emotional effect it had on all of us and our psyches. Disco was the cure we had been looking for without even knowing it. Suddenly, as if an oasis in the desert of Boston, emerged that carefree, hands in air, amyl-nitrate-popper enhanced condition that took a musical high and elevated it to a greater mental and physical one as well.

Thank GOD for the dance music and for the fact that it became a gateway, a sort of ethereal drug and entrance into a safe haven where we nurtured our souls and opened our attitudes to accept change in all ways. We had made the unconscious effort to just enjoy each other as people, not see each other as adversaries or misfits. With the music as catalyst, we could be blind to skin color. We just focused on the eyes of like-minded people and realized they were more like us than not. Don't get me wrong—the music as a starting point had its issues as well, especially in the early dance music scene where it could be cliquish and cultish. And yet that bridge between worlds was still there in a way it hadn't been before.

It wasn't an accident that Disco conquered the world of music in the seventies and beyond and stole the hearts and minds of myriads of clubgoers of all colors, races, and ethnicities. Disco had that special something that allowed it to become the ultimate melting pot for a new age of compromise and reconciliation, and we as the beneficiaries of that wonderful scene were just grateful that we had it. We were grateful too that we had found a sound that belonged to no one else, one that would become a path forward to help heal wounds and make friendships. If the times we lived in had the feeling of an open, oozing wound, then Disco was the balm to help heal it. But it was a balm you had to apply yourself in a time and town that could be alienating, and it could be hard for anyone to transition out of the old ways.

No one needed to tell me what it was like to feel as if you had to prove yourself. I stood in the paradoxical position of being a young white man spinning records and programming the music for the number one black club in New England, the Rhinoceros in Boston. I knew firsthand how fragile that scene was. I struggled to be accepted by an audience that had no reason to trust me, much less follow me. But they would, and once I got established in my own way, I got to play the music that no one else could. And as it turned out, the fact of where I played and what I played helped a young DJ named Joey Carvello, by his own admission, push what was acceptable at his own club, Yesterday. When I met him, he was of the state of mind that he needed to take in as much as possible as fast as he could. From what I could see, he just wanted to be the best and have the freedom to play anything new to an accepting audience, and that's what he was able to get. Albeit after some tension and a boycott.

This book at its core is about a young man whose local roots and upbringing put him at odds with his inner feelings, but by experimentation he pushed through that old barrier and found that no matter the color or sexuality of the individuals he had grown up being told to avoid, everyone had value. In fact, he discovered that all were connected in some way through the one thing that really drove him: the music.

The Boston Hustle is a story about Disco, sure, but it's also a story about awakening, triumph, tragedy, and disappointment. It's finally about betrayal, as the culture and time Joey helped shape were seemingly burned to the ground on a dreadful day in July of 1979 in Comiskey Park. On that day, between doubleheader games of the Chicago White Sox and Detroit Tigers, a Disco-hating fool named Steve Dahl, backed by indie promoters and record labels who couldn't control that music, orchestrated the riot known as Disco Demolition Night. Dahl had them bring all their Disco records to the game to be piled up and burned, to the delight of thousands of uneducated fools who didn't realize they were burning down the one thing that really could and did unite people at that time. Fortunately for all of us, they only burned the vinyl that afternoon, but the movement and the love lived on and rose from those ashes—and is still alive and well today!

If you think creative liberties were taken to enhance the stories inside this book, or that these things could not have happened the way they are recounted, then think twice. I can say for a fact that this crazy, implausible recounting of events was real because I'm John "TC" Luongo, and I lived through it. I saw it all in real time as it happened right in front of me, and, fortunately, I'm still standing, in spite of knowing Joey Carvello for decades more than I'd like to admit.

—John "TC" Luongo

Chapter 1:

TAKA BOOM

I was standing at the edge of the neighborhood, about to make a move nobody had ever pulled around here before. Taka Boom was beside me, relaxed and smiling. But I didn't share the feeling. I was too busy casing the block to see what we were in for.

The action was on an upswing today because of the Feast. It was the first Saturday of September, 1979, which made it the Feast of Saints Cosmas and Damian, the patrons of East Cambridge, Massachusetts. These guys successfully grafted the leg of a dead Ethiopian onto a priest back in the two hundreds, which also made them the patron saints of barbers and bakers. But today I was here for a totally different kind of miracle.

Ahead, the streets were brimming with Wise Guys, Grease Balls, and Goombahs. I spotted the usual crew lined up in front of Joey Mac's like birds on a wire in bad ties and shiny suits. A couple of them were on "souseech and peppah sangwiches" throwing down the double bite: one bite then another without pulling away. There was Cappy, Bomber, Saipan, Joe Chicken, Beppo, Blacky, and Tippy. These guys stood out here almost every day, reading the Race Form and waiting to be called to run a neighborhood "errand," which might have ranged from picking up pizza to driving the get-away car.

My cousin, Alex "Bobo" Petricone, liked to hang out here too. One minute he was minding his business, and the next he was setting off the Irish Gang Wars when somebody slapped his girl's ass. After it had all cleared up, he headed to Hollywood, changed his name to Alex Rocco, and eventually made it big as Moe Green in *The Godfather*; he even did voice-over work for *The Simpsons*.

Meanwhile, the wise guys ahead of us were still playing babootz, the Italian version of rock-paper-scissors, and buying food from the local carts. You could get every kind of festival food off a cart here today, except for meatballs. Italians around here only ate those from reputable sources like their mother, or very close relatives of their mother, so nobody even bothered trying to sell them.

From where we stood, we could hear the Roma Band playing the same beat over and over again. No wonder it was called the Italian death march. The average guy might have heard that music and considered it an omen, especially if that guy was about to take a stroll through this neighborhood with a gorgeous black chick on his arm. To my knowledge, not a single black soul had ever walked through this neighborhood before. But I wasn't going to let that bother me. I grew up in East Cambridge; so did my whole family. As a matter of fact, everybody I knew grew up here.

East Cambridge was literally the other side of the tracks, and we were some tough-ass motherfuckers too—kids from East Cambridge ate hammers for dessert. But aside from a few gang hits every once in a while—and the fact that Mr. Softie wouldn't drive through because when he did he got jacked—the biggest problem was intolerance, which was pretty much the status quo for neighborhoods back then. I wouldn't even really call it a problem, per se, because generally people stayed away from East Cambridge. So I guess it was my problem because I was the one about to take that walk.

I was head of the Boston Record Pool, and Taka's single "Night Dancin'" was getting some good looks in the clubs then. Her manager introduced us, and we hit it off immediately; then he asked if I could take her around town. He probably meant for me to take her to a few clubs or a nice restaurant, but I figured I'd take her to the feast; it would be hilarious!

My family knew that I was in the music business and that my artist list was about 75% black, and that was fine with them because it was a job. But nobody ever expected me to bring my job home—to this neighborhood—with the streets teeming with Italians—during the feast.

Even though Taka was black, some of the Italians in the neighborhood were darker than her. Take my father for example, who, among his many nicknames, was also known as Cigars because that's how dark he was. As opposed to Taka, whose complexion was that of a well-done waffle. She was beautiful, too, with a wild blue, red, and black outfit that was practically painted on, and multicolored hair extensions she wore all the way down to her ass. She dressed the same way she behaved: crazy as a cuckoo clock. It was the good kind of crazy though. Taka was from Chicago, she was Chaka Kahn's little sister, and she could sing her ass off too.

Just then I noticed my little brother, Anthony, heading our way. From the look on his mug, I could see he had spotted me too. He was expertly weaving through the crowd, his eyes darting back and forth between me and Taka. "What ahh you, outta ya mind! What's wrong with you? Where'd you even get her anyway?"

I explained who she was.

"That doesn't make it any better," he said as he spun around to walk beside me.

"I'm about to put some alligators in the pool—let's see how these dopes deal with this shit," I said.

I had already told Taka what the neighborhood was like, but now that she had gotten a good look, she smiled and said, "I'm down, but you sure you want to do this? You have to deal with these people tomorrow. They're your family."

"I know," I said, more confident than ever.

"Well alright," she shrugged her shoulders with a smirk and walked toward the crowds. Anthony fell back as we walked the middle of the street. Once the looks and whispers started, he couldn't take it and moseyed off behind a fried dough stand.

As we passed by Joey Mac's, the birds on a wire started leaning into each other, whispering out loud, saying things like: "What the fuck is he doing?" and, "Cigars must be spinning in his fuckin' grave right now."

But I knew what they were saying wasn't true because my dad wasn't like them. Back in the day when Malcolm X got whacked, all the guys in my neighborhood, myself included, were saying shit like, "Good! They got that spook." My dad heard me talking like an asshole with all the boys and yanked me aside. "You don't know nothin' about that guy except that he was colored. You might want to read up on him and learn what he was about before you spit on his grave and call him a spook," So I did, and wouldn't you know he was assassinated by his own people, a killing instigated by his former mentor, Elijah Muhammad. Another fun fact of which I was unaware was that he had spent seven years in jail right up the street from me at Prison Point in Charlestown. Something in me started to shift then. From that point on, I tore down the barrier in my mind when it came to other people. I listened to and read the preaching of Martin Luther King Jr. Not long after, my friends beat me up and called me a "niggah diggah" because I listened to the Temptations, the Supremes, and my personal favorite, Marvin Gaye. I had to hide my records. How sad is that—those morons—but they were my friends, my family.

As we walked on, without my brother, we heard someone say, *"Disgraciat!"* And then, "What are you doing with that fuckin' *mulignane?* (Mool-in-yahm)"

Taka perked up at that one. "Did he just call me what I think he called me in Italian?"

"No. He called you an eggplant."

"A what? What's an eggplant?"

"I'll show you later. Let's keep it moving. My Auntie Cevita makes the best on the street."

We kept walking through the crowd, which parted like the Red Sea before us now. It felt like even the Roma Band had stopped playing to get a good look. We finally arrived at "the house" where 90% of my aunts, uncles, and cousins lived in a triple-decker across from the Warren Pals Italian American Club. The family was always there, the doors always open from floor to floor, phones ringing, numbers being taken, kids running between rooms. As I approached the house, I saw most of my family standing together in the fenced-in yard. When they got a glimpse of us, several of my aunts ran inside. We heard doors slam and voices in the yard saying: "That crazy *bastahd.* Hide the pocketbooks!"

At that point, my brother surfaced again beside my sisters, Patrice and Barbara. There was no way in hell they were going to miss a second of this. My mother wasn't there, though. She was never around for these things. They tortured that poor lady throughout her whole life because she was Irish, which I couldn't understand because my uncles Frankie and Tony were both married to Irish girls; Cigars wasn't the only one after all.

The remaining relatives and friends who hadn't run away stood posted against the wall of the house facing the street, but nobody said a word to us, and so I started the introductions: "Taka, this is my Auntie Maymay, my Auntie Cevita, my Auntie K, Auntie Anna, and

Auntie Jenny. This is my Uncle Tony." And Tony was, for lack of a better word, as stupid as a stump. He turned his back on her. I just shook my head and moved on down the line.

"This is my Uncle Joe," I said, and Uncle Joe was cool. He had been in the Army and fought at Anzio, and that shit was no joke. He welcomed her. But my Uncle Louie, who was a *strunz*, also turned his back.

At that point, I told her to go give my Uncle Frankie a kiss. Uncle Frankie was the family patriarch. He got things done. If you needed a *No Parking* permit for in front of your house, or your sidewalks fixed, or fifteen cases of frozen hamburgers, Uncle Frankie's line was always the same: "Ok, let me call *the guy*."

She ran up to him, saying, "Uncle Frankie, give me some sugar!" And everyone held their breath. You could hear a mouse piss on cotton. Uncle Frankie turned to run, but she chased him down and kissed his cheek. For a second, I thought that wouldn't go over, but when she did that it was like someone flipped a switch. Uncle Frankie turned and gave her a hug, and then everybody laughed or said, "Awwww."

But then Taka pressed her luck. "Can I use the bathroom?" she asked.

I almost fell down when my Auntie Maymay said, "Of course, honey," and showed her where it was. When Taka came back out of the house, the family was all over her.

"Taka, you want a meatball sandwich?"

"Taka, you want some eggplant?"

"There's that word again," she said. She pronounced it "mul in yan," and the place went bananas.

"Do you know what a *mulignane* is?"

She said, "No. The guys down the street called me that. Joey told me it's a vegetable or a fruit—it's something to eat. I don't know."

"Stay right there. Don't move. Wait for me to come back," someone said. It wasn't unusual for grease balls to make a point in three different phrases. Then someone pulled out a fresh eggplant, and an eggplant is so purple it's almost black. Most of us kind of stepped back to check out how Taka would react. But she almost went to her knees laughing. We all followed.

It was a memorable day because, while the music was my life—and had even saved my life—my family, which was that neighborhood, and my friends and family from the business were separated by an invisible wall every bit as high as The Great Wall of China. But on that Feast of Saints Cosmas and Damian, we shattered that wall. By accepting her, my family accepted me.

Then somebody asked Taka about what kind of music she *did*. "Is it one of Joey's Disco songs?" To them the word "Disco" meant their nephew Joey.

She said, "Yes." And then she said, "Can I sing some for you?"

And they said, "Sure. You can sing. Sing for us."

And she sang for Warren Street. Her voice was so strong it drew people to the fence from the street. She sang for about a minute and a half, and when she was done, they gave her a standing ovation. Of course they were already standing.

There is an expiration date on generosity if a visitor overstays their welcome, so Taka and I soon rolled out on the high note. It could have only gone downhill from there. When we left, they gave her the warmest goodbye I've ever seen a non-family member get from the Carvellos, the Salvias, the Ughetties, and the Morettis.

As we left and walked up the street, people said: "Hey girlie, you can sing." And, "Hey girlie, come back some other time." Everyone was nice except for those birds on a wire. They turned their fat bastard backs on us as we walked by. Then of course my brother all of a sudden joined up with us, walking down the street waving to everybody like he was dynamite, like he actually did something, which he didn't.

"Where you been, you fake tuff guy?" I said and shook my head with a smirk and feigned disgust. Anthony just smiled. He looked up to me even more since I'd made it in the record business.

But the fact that I had made it anywhere outside of jail or the mob was a miracle.

Chapter 2:

EAST CAMBRIDGE

It was summer, 1967. Artie "Woo Woo" Ginsberg was playing "Apples, Peaches, Pumpkin Pie" by Jay and the Techniques through my battery powered AM radio. The boys and I were sitting in the rickety bleachers of Thorndike Park in East Cambridge watching Portuguese people from the neighborhood string up nets on the field.

We had no idea what game they were planning on playing.

After a few minutes, my buddy Joe Pacelli said, "I think that's soccer."

I looked and nodded. "Whatever it is, they're doing it on our field!"

These guys were wearing little shorts with metal cleats and taking forever to string the nets, and there were a shitload of little hooks to connect before they could start.

Prior to seeing them set up, we had wondered what the posts were meant for in the first place. The city had put them up earlier that summer. We were baffled then because they were all wrong for playing football—that is, *real* football—and they had no use standing at the edge of our baseball diamond the way they were. So watching these guys install the net unraveled a mystery for us.

We had gotten used to the Irish, but now the Portuguese lived on Hurley Street. And these people somehow got the city to put up soccer posts at opposite ends of our baseball field. Times were changing.

But East Cambridge wasn't a place for different kinds of people in our minds. That was our park: it was for baseball, it was for football, it was for bottle rockets and homemade bombs; not for these guys in their shorts and their *soccer*.

We didn't even consider soccer a sport then. For first generation Italians, soccer was their thing; they'd read about it in the Italian papers at the Warren Pals Italian American Club. But that sport just didn't filter up to the second generation. And any sport we didn't understand was a *fag* sport.

Still, these boys had to be tough, playing on that dusty, dried-out field littered with broken bottles, rocks, beer cans, and car parts.

After they finished their net, we sat watching them and trying to understand what it was they were doing as they ran around in shorts. At first, we thought it would be like hockey because of the nets, but they didn't even score. They just ran around.

We didn't make a move while they played. A few times they looked over at us. But as far as they knew, we were just a bunch of kids listening to AM radio. Little did they know we had every intention of bothering them (a neighborhood pastime).

When they left, they made the mistake of leaving the nets in place, and we burned them to the ground after they were out of sight. I remember looking at the scorched poles when the fires were out and wondering if we should get rid of those too.

Soon after that, our Portuguese neighbors put up another pair of nets. Instead of burning these, we just cut them down. The last little blaze had brought the fire department to the neighborhood asking questions. And we didn't need more trouble than we already had, so going forward, a razor was all we needed. It didn't attract undue attention. After we had cut the nets several times, the Portuguese went and put up metal ones. So we got bolt cutters and cut those down as well. But these guys still wanted to play soccer, and so they started taking the nets with them and putting them up for the game, which took about twenty minutes. They really worked at it too. They must've loved soccer to go through all that trouble.

I had to feel a bit of respect for their resilience; even still, I didn't care.

For a while that summer, we didn't see the nets anymore. We thought they had given up, but then Joe Pacelli missed church one Sunday and saw what they were up to. They had started playing again, but this time on Sunday mornings, probably to avoid us.

The next weekend, we skipped church just to visit with them. You could tell they were weary when they saw us arrive. And while they wouldn't have known which neighborhood boys had been cutting their nets down, I'm sure we looked like prime candidates. These guys were older too, and there were about thirty of them. There were only five of us and some of the Irish kids, but we didn't give a fuck. It was like how water buffalo move in a herd on the savannas and feel safe, except in the distance hyenas are waiting. There are fewer hyenas, but the buffalo have to keep an eye on them or else a hyena will take one of them out.

That's just how we thought we were supposed to be. We were protecting the neighborhood and living up to the myth behind it. People thought if you went to East Cambridge you were going to take a beating, and so most people stayed away.

There were other reasons people stayed away from the neighborhood too. The Cambridge blue bloods, the Harvard Square WASPS, kept out because we lived where the city hid some of its ugliness. Here we had toxic waste dumps, a lumberyard, a slaughterhouse, and one of the last fresh-kill chicken places that I knew of in New England; it was called "Fresh Kills." They sold T-shirts with their name on them. There was even green shit coming out of the ground by where the Boston Hose Company had its building. And all that dumped into the tributaries that flowed into the Charles River.

On top of these wonderful features, of course, there was us.

For this last reason, the blue bloods changed the route of the Head of the Charles Regatta races so they didn't have to go through East Cambridge anymore. The Charles River separated Cambridge from Boston. On our side of the river, East Cambridge basically ran the stretch between the Massachusetts Avenue Bridge and the Longfellow Bridge. In the beginning, the rowers raced all the way under the Massachusetts Avenue Bridge and then turned around and went back. Everybody would line up on both sides of the river to watch. The Cambridge patricians with their deck shoes, fancy hats, and pipes would come early to get good seats and converse about their relatives on the Mayflower or about Thoreau, or whatever it was they talked about.

But then we came along and bothered the shit out of those people. We'd take a piss next to the Brahmin in the smoking jacket or snag a fish with treble hooks from the river and throw it in the street where the cars would run it over and splatter the guts. "How's that smell in the sun?"

One thing we loved to do was to bother people, like with the Portuguese or with anybody else. It wasn't personal. It was like a lifestyle in the neighborhood. And the only people we loved to bother more than each other were outsiders. I'd come home and my father would ask me what I had done that day.

"I bothered a few people."

"Did you get in trouble?"

"No."

The regatta gave us the opportunity to bother people we seldom got the opportunity to see, and it allowed us to play our favorite game: throwing explosives at the racers.

When the rowers came toward us from the bridge, they were in the middle of the river. We couldn't hit them out there; they were too far away. But that little fact didn't stop us. As soon as they came into sight, we threw Cherry Bombs or M-80s in their general direction. That first bang would echo over the river like the shot heard 'round the world. Spectators flinched like they were caught in a crossfire, until they realized what we were doing. The people along the course didn't even bother trying to stop us. Muffy and Buffy were no match for the kids from East Cambridge. But sooner or later, we knew the police were coming. It was part of the festivities. We had lookouts posted. The police were Met cops who were part of the Cambridge police force and also part of the MIT police. They didn't like us at all. And they had no ties to our neighborhood or its politics and power. In fact, the MIT cops were paid to bother us.

We threw explosives at the rowers for like two or three years, and then one year the race didn't come through East Cambridge anymore. To avoid our fireworks display at the tail end of the course, the WASPS just extended the beginning of the race further west up the Charles.

We altered their regatta and were proud of it.

We weren't exactly choirboys, even though we went to church every Sunday. And in the neighborhood, these fresh Portuguese émigrés were vastly outnumbered by the Italians.

So now it was Sunday morning. The Portuguese had come down to play at this time to avoid us. But there we were. They saw us sitting off to the side but went on with their game anyhow. What were some Italians and a few Irish boys going to do anyways?

Even though East Cambridge was Italian, there were still a bunch of Irish around. The Burkes had like 17 kids. Papa Burke was a real Catholic: no condoms. And the Tumeys were local and as Irish as it gets. One of their kids became mayor, one chief of police, and the other a monsignor. Now that's Irish.

That morning, we let the Portuguese soccer boys play until they broke for halftime. At that point, someone gave the sign, and we sprinted onto the field, knocking a couple of guys down before they knew what was going on. Scuffles broke out across the field, and while the players were occupied, I grabbed the black and white ball, and we all ran away. At that point, they chased us out into the road and down the street, but once we got to Thorndike Street they pulled up short, their cleats screeching against the pavement as they stopped. They had come to the line that marked the edge of *our* East Cambridge. Here we would get protection and back up, and they would catch a sad beating. There was no way Italians were going to let a bunch of Portuguese beat us in our own streets—didn't matter what we did.

At that point, they stopped short and just looked at us. We looked back at them across the street, both groups knowing where we stood. Then I knifed the soccer ball and threw the flat ball back. They swore at us in Portuguese, and we laughed. We owned that neighborhood, and, grown men or not, they knew it.

At this point, we were done bothering them, and the hyenas went to go find the next victim. It would have kept up like that too. But one night there was a fire on the end of Hurley Street in a triple-decker. An Italian, an Irish, and a Polish family lived in that building (not a joke). It was a late night/early morning fire at the end of the street on which the Portuguese lived. When the building went up, some of our new Portuguese neighbors ran in there and led people out of the fire. It didn't make a difference if they were Italian or Irish, they ran in there and got them out.

From that point on, the Portuguese were part of the family. They were as good as Italian. They had made their bones, and I saw them as people for the first time, not just "Geese," which was what we had called them.

That was the beginning of the change in my worldview. If it got a little broader at that moment, I still had a long way to go if I was ever going to avoid hard prison time and neighborhood errands, but I was coming around to the idea at least that I would have to grow beyond my neighborhood.

But growing out of my neighborhood wasn't going to happen overnight, and in the meantime, I would make the friends who would make Disco happen with me.

CHAPTER 3:

THE NATIONAL GUARD

Ricky Maciejko. He was a big guy: six-foot-three, two-thirty. He had his own car too, and the newest music. I met him the day Joe Pacelli from Thorndyke Street had taken me over to Patsy's for the first time to hang out. It wouldn't be the last.

We were still in High School. The place was a teen hangout on the corner of 9th and Otis. The owner, Patsy, was a big, heavy guy who lived upstairs with his mother. He had a jukebox and a pinball machine inside, where he sold some food and candy. We'd go there to smoke cigarettes. And as long as you were buying something from him, you could hang out in front.

I remember there were stairs in the shop leading to the living area above. At the bottom of the stairs was a sunny landing where a huge beagle named Bella used to lie. Then one day Patsy's mother tripped and fell down the stairs, and that poor dog broke her fall. We heard it from out front as she went: a sudden thud, and one loud and pained "WOOF!" Patsy ran to the stairs and helped his mother back up. That's when we noticed the dog was dead. Died in the line of duty.

We all just went back out in front of the store and spent another afternoon eating ice cream, smoking cigarettes, and bothering each other, and we left the dog to Patsy.

We still had high school to protect us from the real world after all, but that wouldn't last. And as soon as I graduated, I knew I couldn't just hang out in the neighborhood or at Patsy's forever.

My only productive racket then was Tae Kwon Do. One of the older guys from the neighborhood had taken up martial arts, and I followed suit. The biggest surprise to me and anyone who knew me was that I earnestly looked up to the tough-as-nails Korean man that ran the school. Lucky for me, he loved me and nicknamed me Italian Joe. I was an exceptional student: practiced, efficient, and skilled enough that I could break as many boards as the black belts long before I earned one. I did that too. I even managed to make it into some tournaments held in New York City. A notable moment for me was watching my opponent get into the ring and perform a lengthy Kung Fu dance. I'm not sure if he was doing it to entertain the crowds or to intimidate me, but it didn't matter. I waited for him to stop and then kicked him in the face. And I had a nasty kick. But Tae Kwon Do wasn't going to save me from myself.

The draft was on then too, so in order to avoid that, which most likely would have sent me to Vietnam, I joined the National Guard. My thinking was that I could stay on the streets and avoid "the Nam," but, as usual, my best ideas got me into the worst jams. I spent several months as a weekend warrior at Fort Devens, shooting guns, doing drugs, and chasing girls, until one day our platoon deployed to Harvard Square to keep the peace in an anti-war protest. As much as I enjoyed raising hell, I wasn't about to start smacking people around who felt the same way I did.

"Fuck this," I said after that weekend and stopped going altogether. This whole National Guard thing was also a big inconvenience, and I had other things to do, like hanging with Ricky and the Geraneos, drinking Boone's Farm, smoking weed, chasing skirts, and completing a crash course in breaking and entering. Allegedly.

Obviously, I was unaware of the repercussions one faces by blowing off obligations to the United States of America. Bad shit happens when you don't read the handbook.

One afternoon I was working my patronage job at the printing press in Cambridge City Hall, the Mayor just upstairs, when two armed MPs came in and drug my ass out. Right into the Army I went. There was no chance to have a sit-down, no chance for me to do the Scooby-Doo and come up with an excuse. I was out of there. No trial. No time to get my shit together.

I thought for sure I was going to Vietnam, or, at the least, an outpost in East Bumfuck. But the Army called my parents and told them to send my personal belongings to Fort Dix, New Jersey, where they processed me and gave me a Korean haircut—you know, where it's short on top but they buzz the sides all around. After that, they let me call my mother. At that point, I added to the list she was already sending by having her include my military wig in the package.

I had gotten the wig to pass short hair regulations in the National Guard, which was another wonderful idea on my part. When I found out that wigs were tolerated in the Guard as long as you didn't make a problem or cause aggravation, I bought myself one. Now that I knew I was going to be in for the long haul, I wanted to be sure to have it my way, and growing my hair back and hiding it with a wig was at the top of the list, but I had to feel it out first.

From Dix, they put me on a plane and sent me to Huntsville, Alabama, where a guy in a military Jeep picked me up and drove me to the Redstone Arsenal. By the looks of the base, it was obviously a loose place. There were plenty of clues that let me know discipline was not strong here: dull, unpolished boots, bushy non-regulation mustaches, and longer hair to name a few. Right then I knew that if I put the wig on, everybody would just think that was how I looked.

On the wig went, and I presented myself to the CO with my cap over the wig.

The commanding officer's name was John Kennedy, strangely enough a home comfort, but familiarity ended with his name. He proceeded with the customary rhetoric, a speech passed up most likely from my kindergarten teacher to anyone who had any direct authority over me, "Stay out of trouble, blah blah blah." Followed by, "Keep your nose clean."

The only difference between this lecture and the two hundred identical ones I had received throughout my life was that this one was missing any and all traces of a Boston accent. Therefore, I took it less seriously. But just when I was about to doze off, he said something that made my ears perk up: "You're gonna get your own quarters."

I practically fell out of my chair. How were they going to give me my own room? That would put me in the perfect position to get into a lot of trouble. Apparently, they were making me a clerk's typist, and getting my own room went with the gig. Maybe Uncle Frankie had something to do with that too. I already wondered why they hadn't put a gun in my hand and sent me to the jungles. Then Kennedy introduced me to the post's Master Sergeant who processed me in.

"This is a loose base," the Master Sergeant said, which was more proof I had carte blanche. "Your time will go by quick. Before you know it, you'll be back home fucking those I-talian chicks. But if you fuck up, you fuck up for everybody. I got it good here. I did my time in "The Nam." I don't need any more fucking trouble. And you don't want to give me any trouble, do you, Car-a-velli?" They never got my name right. It was obvious there weren't a lot of Italians, or as they called us, "I-talians" on base.

"No, sir." I said.

And he snapped back at me, "Sir, don't call me sir. I work for a living."

When he was done with his talk, I felt good. This was better than I thought. After all, our motto as clerk's typists was: "We don't retreat, we backspace." And on top of that, this was an easy base.

Once I had settled in and surveyed my new home, I headed for the mess hall, which was open until nine. After a few minutes inside the hall, it dawned on me that the room was all whites. At this point I started wondering, "Where are all the brothers?" I had already been on base for a few hours and had yet to see a single black face. This was the '70s, and we had officially gone from calling black people coloreds, to negroes, to black, and now it was brothers. And that's what I was wondering as I looked around. This was the South after all, and a kid from Boston thinks of black people coming from the South. But this was also the Deep South, and shit hadn't changed that much down here.

No matter how racist we thought Boston was (and it was), relations there were downright pleasant compared to how it was down here. I had also amended my views of other people since the days of bothering the Portuguese in the neighborhood. I had sold angel dust in Boston before coming here, and that put me in touch with all kinds of people. I'd learned the only color most people saw was green, and that blacks, or brothers, were just people like anybody else. I had also been busy listening to what a lot of people still thought of as black music. And I had had a couple of fights to support my views in the neighborhood. I'll tell you one thing, anybody who knew me, or knew of me, ever called me a *niggah diggah*.

So here I was on this base in Alabama, where blacks and whites still had separate facilities. In the barracks, whites slept downstairs and the blacks upstairs. The place more or less had a "back of the bus" feel. There was no co-mingling, and I was bothered by how segregated it was. It was East Cambridge magnified a hundredfold. Even though the civil rights movement was in full swing, Huntsville hadn't gotten the memo. And the racism here was blatant, unlike in the North where it was hypocritical. In Boston, they'd be nice to your face and call you a n****r behind your back. But down here they'd call you n****r right to your face.

I finished in the mess hall, so I headed to the rec room where there was a pool table. There, I was shocked to see three black guys playing. One of them was sitting down, another was shooting, and the third was waiting his turn with the cue in his hand. When I walked up, they all turned and looked at me. I didn't know who was squirming more, me or them. We stood there just looking each other over, not sure of what to make of the situation. This was one of the few moments in my life where I was the only white guy in a room and was uncomfortable.

I figured I'd break the ice. I said, "How you guys doin'?"

The guy who was sitting down said, "We're fine, we're fine, you want to play?"

The guy who was shooting put his cue down and said, "We're done playing."

"No," I said and gave him an inquisitive look. "Keep playing."

"Thank you," the two guys said and kept going.

But the guy standing with a cue in his hand didn't say a word. He stood there leaning on it and looked at me like to let me know, "I'm not one of them." I took it to mean he wasn't from the South. I wanted to find out more about him. He seemed like someone I might want to know. But before I could say anything, the door swung open, and I heard: "What the fuck are you n****rs doing here? Get the fuck out." That blew my mind. Two white guys walked toward us. They were real shit-kickers too. The one in the lead, who had spoken when he entered, was bigger than his partner and walked with a hillbilly swagger I hadn't seen before. I knew by looking at him that this was going to be trouble.

The two brothers shooting pool put down their cues and looked to the Northern brother as if to say: "What do we do?" He didn't move.

Then that Southern shit-kicker walked up to the guy still holding the cue and tried to snatch it from him. When he didn't let it go right away, the shit-kicker said, "N****r, you don't want it from me, do you, boy?" When he said that, the other two just walked away.

That's when I shouted, "YO!" And everybody turned to look at the I-talian guy with the Boston accent yelling from the side of the table. If anything could have been worse than a black guy to these shit-kickers, it would have been a Yankee, Italian Catholic from Boston. I might have been the antichrist. The Klan handed out pamphlets on people like me.

As they registered what I was, I said, "Give him the cue back!"

There was no confusing where I stood now. I looked to the two guys headed for the door and said: "You guys don't have to go. You guys play." Then I turned to the redneck and his minion and said, "You get the fuck outa here right fu-ck-ing now!"

"What the fuck are you? When did you get here? This is my God dammed pool hall," the lead redneck said in an unusual but familiar Southern accent. It was creole. So I knew he was from Louisiana.

"Fuck you. Not anymore." I said. "This is my pool hall."

He looked at me then and smiled—a real sick smile. "I guess we got a real n****r lovin' Yankee on our hands."

He came toward me then.

"What did you just say?" I said. He was about arm's length in front of me.

"I called you a nigg..." he said, but before he got the "er" out of his mouth, I kicked him in the face. I hit him so cleanly under the chin that his lights went out and he slid forward down the pool cue into an awkward pile on the floor. The things you can learn from a tough old Korean man in East Cambridge might surprise you. When he hit the floor, I turned and looked at his minion. Tears came to his eyes, and I saw his knees buckle. I had just knocked out the post bully, and he knew he didn't stand a chance.

The two other brothers just sat down. The third one, the tough guy, didn't change his expression. He stood there, observing me. At the same time, we glanced over toward the sound of the dunce coming to on the floor.

I leaned down to him and rolled him over: "You wanna know who I am?" I said. "My name is Joe Carvello. These guys are my friends. If you ever fuck with them again, I'll give you another beating." I turned around and said, "I don't know what's going on down here. But I ain't into this shit. And if any of you guys have a problem, you let me know. I'm not one of these ignorant assholes. And besides that I'm not white, I'm Italian, there's a huge difference." They didn't know how to take that last part.

The tough black guy said, "You didn't have to do that, man."

I said, "No problem, brother."

He said, "I ain't your brother," and walked out. I am pretty sure he called me a Dego under his breath. To be honest, I liked his style.

The next day that guy I knocked out was looking for me all over the barracks. He was leaning into barracks' windows and shouting, "Where is that Yankee n****r lover?" He didn't remember my name. I heard him calling me, so I came out of my little room.

"You looking for me?" I asked.

"Yeah, I'm looking for you."

"You want to do it again?" I said.

Before he could lift his hands, I had the heel of my foot in his chin. He went down just the same as the night before.

"Damn, what are you, one of those chink, Bruce Lee, karate motherfuckers?" He said from his knees. When he said that I hit him with an open hand slap that cracked on his face like lightning.

"What the fuck is wrong with you, dude? Who are you and why are you such an asshole?" I said.

"My name is Richard Proctor."

"I'm pretty sure you don't remember what I said to you last night 'cause you were sleeping, but my name is Joe Carvello." I asked him where he was from, and he told me, "New Orleans." We actually became friends. I bonded with him in that moment for some reason. Maybe I took him on as a project. Or maybe I just wanted to understand him. On top of that, I knew he was nuts, and I liked that. I also knew he was a tough motherfucker, and he was well-connected on the post.

After that, we went to my room and smoked a joint. He had weed, and that was good. He knew about girls in the area too, and he had all the best drugs and knew the hot spots off base. But I did make one thing clear to him right up front: "Listen, I'm not going to preach to you, but you just can't say n****r—you just can't use it around me. It's just gonna piss me off."

"What about porch monkey?"

"What the fuck is wrong with you?"

"You know I could kick your ass if you gave me a chance," he said.

"Now why would I give you a chance to kick my ass? Not only are you a racist, you're a dumb fuck too. I'll tell you what," I said. "You feel like you got a chance, take it."

Sure enough, when I turned around to leave, he bashed me in the back of my head and opened up a can of gumbo whoop ass. When I got up from the floor, he said, "Opportunity knocked, motherfucker."

I told him that he would never take me face to face, never. He tried it again and again. And as much as he tried was as much as he got his ass kicked.

Despite the fighting, Proctor and I started smoking and selling weed together on a regular basis. At first we were smalltime, just buying joints here and there on post, but after a short while we went halves on our first deal together and sold it on base. The profit was good enough that it paid for what we smoked. But soon a little birdie told us who the guy we bought from was getting his shit from, and we put the middleman out of business. After that, we sold to everybody: officers, cooks, barbers...rocket scientists. That post was basically stoned all the time, and we were supplying them.

Soon it was time to take it to the next level. "Why don't we just buy in pounds?" I said. And that's what we did.

Our connection was in Birmingham, Alabama. Soon we got a room in a house off-post with this rich nerd of a guy stationed at the same base, just in a different barrack. He'd buy weed from us just to smoke with us, and he drove a Hemi Challenger—an orange Cuda—and of course he had the spot, while we had the girls and the drugs. Together we made the perfect team.

Then somebody asked me for acid. I figured, "why not?" So I picked up some "double dome orange sunshine" and some "mister natural" and some other shit I don't even remember the name of. We supplied every drug the base needed. We even got our hands on this stuff called Placidyl, a hypnotic sedative that causes euphoria and basically knocked you on your ass. Literally, it put people in comas. It was pretty addictive and was eventually taken off the market. A little insight into just how insane Proctor was: one night he started a fight with me while he was on Placidyl. I couldn't believe it—he was practically unconscious and still violent.

I was selling all that inventory and making plenty of money. And it wasn't long before I loved life on that base. But like any other "too good to be true" thing, my time was coming to an end. Proctor shortly got word he was going to be transferred off-post. But we had enough time for one last Saturday night.

The last night with Proctor, we went to a local bar to celebrate. That's when I got introduced to a bona fide deejay.

This place usually had a jukebox in the corner playing music, but when I walked in, I noticed that the jukebox was off and there was a deejay with two turntables going. At that moment, he was playing "China Grove" by the Doobie Brothers. But as he faded out the song, he started the next record right over the fade. I thought, "Wow, that's a good idea. There's no gap between the songs that way. Shit, I can do that." I was used to playing record hops in the Hully Gully Hall back in East Cambridge. When I'd switch records to put on another 45, I would take requests, but people would get off the dance floor when the music stopped, and you'd always have to get them back. The way this deejay was doing it, the music never stopped, and people didn't leave the floor. I knew I was going to try that technique.

As I was running through the implications, Richard Proctor turned and said to me, "How about one more for the road?"

We both stood. I knuckled him. He went down but got right up and bashed me with a chair. Some guy tried to jump in, but we both turned on him. Then everybody jumped in and started fighting. Suddenly there were barstools and punches and bottles being thrown everywhere. Somebody hit me, and my lip was cut open. I looked over and Richard's nose was gushing blood. Then the MPs charged in, dragging people out and cuffing them. But they didn't arrest us. Most of those MPs got their drugs and girls from our house. You don't put your best connection in jail, do you? We were basically off-limits.

The next day, I watched Proctor board the bus to leave. I was beginning to think he had changed his views, but then he looked back from the door and said with a smile, "Goodbye you n****r, spook, porch-monkey loving, Dego, grease ball, WOP motherfucker," and then he winked.

He said goodbye to me the way he said hello. I never saw or talked to him again after that.

I kept the business going after he left. I even put together some integrated card games that had one rule: "I don't want to hear any of that n****r shit, and I don't want to hear any honky or Casper shit either. That's the way my parties are, and if you don't like it, then go back to the fucking bayou or the mountains or the bricks or wherever you motherfuckers learned to walk upright!"

Nobody disagreed with me.

I had put the whole thing together within a year. My vision of what a club should be began in that time and at those parties in the Army. Good music, good drugs, and good people all together and getting along. At that point, I used the drugs and girls I had to make these parties happen. It hadn't dawned on me yet that all I needed were some turntables and a room, and maybe some drinks, and I could make the same thing come together without the threat of jail time.

Of course it was all about to unravel.

One weekend shortly after Proctor left, a new guy showed up on post. He was a real stoner. For lack of a better term, he was a "military hippie." He approached me. "I know your partner's gone. If you need any help, I'm your guy," he said.

"What the fuck are you talking about?"

"Well, I heard that you're the guy." I thought of Uncle Frankie when he said that.

"Wrong guy."

He said, "Let's go smoke a joint." I went with him, but I still played dumb.

But I didn't play dumb for long enough. We started hanging out together after that. His name was Maxwell something or other. After about a month, I brought him into the business.

I took him to Birmingham with me one night for a quick run to pick up a couple of pounds. The plan was to drop it off at the apartment, go back to the post, then head to the pad and have it all broken up to sell over the weekend.

But on the way back to Birmingham, Maxwell was complaining that he felt sick, so instead of taking him to the spot off-base, I took him back to the barracks and brought the weed with me. When I dropped him off, I took a couple of Placidyls and, feeling sleepy, went to sleep clutching a pound of weed under each arm and a bag of 500 Placidyl on my chest.

All I remember is light shining in my face, and then my blanket came off, and there I was clutching all those drugs like a teddy bear.

"We finally fucking got you, Caravelli," someone laughed.

They put me in the post's stockade, where I stayed for forty-eight hours. From there, I was told I was going to Leavenworth. I eventually found out that Maxwell was actually CID (Central Intelligence Division).

"Motherfucker!" I said to myself more than once.

When I told my mother about what had happened, she started crying. My father got on the phone; he had a lot to say to me, but he ended with, "Uncle Frankie... he knows a guy." All that time, I still had that wig on in the stockade, waiting for sentencing and a long bid.

Then, about three weeks away from my trial, the CO called me in. I was fucked.

When I walked in, the CO said, "I don't know how the fuck you did it. But you're out. They dropped the charges. You're going home tomorrow." He smirked, "You're taking a bus back."

I didn't get a dishonorable discharge. I got what they called an "undesirable discharge," which means a discharge with no military benefits.

Next day came and the bus arrived. I walked off the post and through the fence to the street where the bus was waiting. All the COs were lined up to watch me leave. But when I got to the foot of the stairs leading onto the bus, I turned and pulled off my wig and let my long hair fall out. I was outta that motherfucker, and they couldn't do shit about it.

My timing would prove to be impeccable. The Discotheques were just about to explode, and I was coming home to assist.

CHAPTER 4:

ZELDA

It was January '74.

I had been out of the army now for just over a year and hadn't been doing much of anything but hitting different local clubs in East Cambridge and avoiding jail. But on this night, we were going outside our comfort zone to the other side of the river and the hottest club in Boston: Zelda.

The first thing we noticed in front of the club were the cars—cleaned, waxed, and gleaming under the streetlights. We stopped, mouths open, and watched through the roll-down windows. There I saw a Mercedes 230 SL, an out of the showroom Cadillac Baritz, and then up pulled a white '71 Grand Prix convertible with red interior and red soft top. Out of the car stepped a big guy in great shape, with a porn star blond mustache, and a blond, vent brushed hairdo. He was wearing an outstanding skin-tight Jantzen polyester shirt. He also wasn't wearing any pants.

The people in the line just looked at him as he stepped onto the curb in boxer shorts. "What's going on, John?" someone called out.

Then he took his pressed pants from the back seat and put them on, looked up and said, "Keeps the creases out of the backs of the legs. I don't like creases."

I was thinking, "What the fuck?"

We were at a real Discotheque now, there was no mistaking that. Before this, the clubs we had been going to had puke on the floor, twenty-five cent beers, and a live band. The whores in tube tops and flip-flops were everywhere. Compared with that scene, Zelda was a quantum leap. The guys in line were dressed like movie stars. While the world I knew was a brown pair of shoes, Zelda was a tuxedo.

And if I liked the way the men were dressed, the women were just beautiful. I had never seen their style, not even in catalogues or in movies. I was used to the mod look or the Woodstock look for chicks, but this was a whole new world. I just said, "Wow," and shook my hand like I was brushing something off my coat—it was a grease-ball move. And this was all based on the drive-by—we hadn't even got inside the club yet.

The front of the place was black, and the awning was the same, with white piping and the *Zelda* logo. It was the first club I had been to with an awning. To us that was class.

Carl, Ricky, Frankie, and I drove on looking for parking and ended up five blocks away. That was the crew. I had met Carl Lupo back in '71 while he was working the Feast for his Uncle Patsy. There was a secondary leg of the Feast on 9th Street, and Patsy used to set up a stand there in front of his store. I had known Carl from back in high school. We never talked then, but after we got acquainted at the Feast, we quickly became friends and started hanging out. I would print our fake IDs at my City Hall job, and Carl started bringing out his cousin, Frank De Pasquale (Frankie D.), who lived by St. Mary's in Cambridge.

Now that I had gotten back from the Army and was safe from Leavenworth, we were hanging out all the time again. But this was our first exposure to Boston nightlife. And that was true in more than one sense, since we never dressed for the weather, and it was cold out that night. We just rolled out in our pleather jackets, flared poly blend slacks, and polyester shirts, and ran to the club with our hands in our pockets. As we passed the door and all the people waiting, we could smell all the colognes. I was using Canoe and English Leather or Jade East back then, which was the usual in the Italian hamlets, but here I smelled all these fragrances I never knew before. These new smells set the whole scene for me, the way the smell of fresh bread sets a bakery. It smelled like Disco. And I forgot all about the cold.

We hit Zelda that first time on a Thursday night. Waiting in line, I noticed there were almost no girls, except those in couples. Couples had to wait, but if a guy showed up with four broads, he got in automatically. A group of good-looking girls didn't wait at all. That meant the girls in line without a date were usually what we called, "ouch." The rest of that line was just guys waiting for their chance like us.

I could tell we didn't belong just by looking around. But after seeing what I had already seen, I didn't want to be any place else, and I thought we at least had a chance because we were dressed right—we all were. We came as correct as we could. We were dynamite for East Cambridge. But who knew what the doorman would say?

Then we saw a guy give the doorman a kiss on the cheek and cuff him what was obliviously a greenback. My friend Frankie D. saw that and said, "You see that? We gotta tip if we want to get in here."

"Here's five bucks," I said.

"Five bucks? Yo, you ain't in East Cambridge anymore and a *finnif* ain't gonna work. We need to hit this guy with a *double, double sawbuck.* We'll split it." There were four of us, so ten bucks apiece was forty bucks, which was a lot of money back then.

We got up to the front and Frankie D. put his hand out and said to the doorman: "How you doing? My name is Frankie D."

The doorman shook Frankie's hand and said, "Fine, Frankie, how you doing?"

It was obvious that Frankie palmed him the forty dollars.

As the doorman peeked into his hand, he said, "How many are you?"

"There's four of us."

He lifted the velvet rope then.

I thought I had just come out to hopefully *gank* a hot broad that night, but it all changed when I got inside. It hit me when I turned the corner and saw my first Disco Ball, which, together with the song they were playing, blew my mind. Zelda's sound system wasn't overwhelming, but it was good enough. Of course, the speakers didn't matter to me that night. The song was "Soul Makossa" by Manu Dibango. It had this unbelievable soul bass, driving over a track I'd never heard anything like before. You know the line "Something moved me;" well, this song moved me. It had a big kick beat with serious attack and a killer alto sax. And it was obviously a crowd favorite because the place was going batshit.

I didn't understand a word that motherfucker was saying, but it didn't matter. Just from hearing it that first time under the lights among all those people was like an out-of-body experience. I was floating toward the music.

All of a sudden, another song seamlessly surfaced without any lag between. The song was: "I'll Always Love My Mama," by the Intruders. I almost fell down. And then right behind it, "Rock the Boat." The next to follow was one of the only Funk records I heard that night. The introduction said, "Ladies and Gentlemen, these are the JBs," and then James Brown came in and said, "Hit it," and the club went crazy. This was by far the funkiest song I had ever heard in my life, called "Doing it to Death." I went down to my knees, and it never stopped.

From there, the music flowed in an unbroken series of unbelievable R&B and Soul songs that I had never heard before. The combination of the lights, the sounds and the crowd jammed on the dance floor at that moment made me feel like I was reincarnated and moving onto my next life. I kept on getting hit with hit after hit after hit. It was nonstop.

The music was controlling the entire atmosphere and movement in the room. I never saw people in such sync with the music. It was like a school of fish. And then I understood the mirrored ball. It was like the ball reflected the people, who in turn mirrored the music.

I looked around. I wanted to know where the music was coming from. Where was the deejay? How was he putting it together? The room was relatively dark, except for this square hole in the wall, which I assumed was the booth. I negotiated my way through the packed dance floor and up to the booth to learn the names of the songs I had just heard.

At the booth, I saw what I had seen in the army with the two turntables, but the songs transitioned flawlessly, much better than I had heard back then. How was this guy doing it? It was perfect. He was mixing the records together like a blender. As I watched him mix, I was paralyzed, except for my ears.

My intention was to ask him the names of the last four or five songs that I'd heard. But then he played another one, and once again my doors got blown off. That's when I said, "Excuse me, what is this?" But the deejay didn't even look up. Once again, I said, "Excuse me, what's the name of this song?" And he responded, "'When the Fuel Runs Out,' by Executive Suite." He seemed annoyed.

"What did you play before that?"

The guy lifted his head again. Just by looking at him, I could tell he thought he was dynamite. I could also tell he was smug and arrogant. I said to myself, "If he looks at me like that for another five seconds, I'm going to punch his face in." But then I had an epiphany. I realized I was talking to the star of the room, and I had better change my approach. So I said, "I love the music you're playing. I can't believe how great you are. Half the songs you play, I haven't heard them. This is my first time here, and I've never seen a deejay play records the way you do."

I figured if I blew smoke up this guy's ass, maybe I could get some information out of him. "What's your name?"

He said, "Andrew."

"Andrew, would you mind telling me the names of a couple of the songs you played?"

"Come back and talk to me later. I'm deejaying right now." He said it like he was performing brain surgery.

About an hour later, I went up to the booth and said, "Hey, it's me again."

"Sorry, I can't talk to you, come see me at the end of the night."

I said, "Ok," but inside I was saying, "What the fuck is your problem, you Crypt Keeper looking motherfucker?"

This attitude that I got from Andrew was prevalent throughout the whole fucking club, and we took offense to it. We weren't being treated badly, but we weren't being treated well either. Who were we after all? It was our first time there; nobody knew who the fuck we were, and we weren't spending the kind of money people were spending at the bar. Beers for a *deuce* blew our mind, which were actually three dollars because they expected a buck tip. And there was no way we could have had cocktails—we would have been out of there in two drinks.

Aside from the attitude, this place was beyond cool. The waitresses were wicked, and the bartenders were dressed like *The Great Gatsby*. Everybody was dressed like it was a competition, a fashion show, and all the waitresses were tens. It was a privilege just to be served by them. There was one particular waitress who was arguably the greatest waitress in the history of the Boston club scene. Her name was Babe. Her real name was Florence Collangelo. She was one of the most beautiful women in Boston. This broad was making

$500 a night, and she only worked one section. I couldn't even order a drink from her if I wanted. She worked the greaseball, East Boston, Revere, North End section. They were the real wise guys and up-and-comers. We couldn't even walk near that section, and there was no velvet rope either—just an imaginary line drawn in the floor that you didn't cross. And if you weren't in that section, the best you could do was watch her walk by, which was worth the extra cost of drinks.

I eventually became good friends with Babe's boyfriend, Michael Chioffi, a.k.a. Chify. Who, when I first met him, was wearing a bad-ass Nik-Nik shirt, had amazing hair, and was sporting a gold necklace with a cross, a Saint Christopher's medal for good luck, an Italian Horn, and a diamond pinky ring. Don't get it twisted: Italians were blinging way before hip-hop gave it the name "bling." And he was going out four nights a week, all hours of the night, and going to law school on top of it. He was a genius from East Boston, which was hard-core Italian, and, as you can imagine, there was a microscopic list of geniuses there. He was surrounded by *strunzs* and *bacallas*, but he passed his bar exam on the first try. It was a Disco miracle.

Another Disco miracle was that my guys couldn't pull a single girl on that dance floor, which was unusual. I saw them go up to chick after chick, where the girls just turned around and walked away. My guys were still using the lines from the puke bars. And my best friend, Carl Lupo, who was our version of Sam Malone, had the best rejection of the night. He walked up to a girl and said, "What happened at Pearl Harbor?"

"I don't know?" she said.

And before she had a chance to finish her sentence, he kissed her on the lips and said, "Sneak attack!" He had done this before, but he'd never gotten a reaction like he was about to get. This girl hauled off and punched him in the face. I thought we were going to get killed. A couple of big guys walked over to Carl then and lifted him up. I was more pissed off that we were going to get kicked out of the place than I was about what was happening to Carl.

The gorillas were headed to the back door with Lupo. Bouncers never threw people out the front; it's not a good look for people in line and the neighbors. Instead, they take you out back where anything can happen, and that's where Carl was headed until the girl he'd bothered saved his ass. She grabbed one of the bouncers and told him the line that Carl had dropped on her. They cracked up, put Carl down, and the chick actually bought him a drink. Carl used that line for the next twenty years and batted about .340. If picking up girls were baseball, Carl was a Hall of Famer.

Once I realized we were going to get to stay, I went back to listening to the music. "What's the name of that song?" I kept saying. I must have said "wow" twenty times.

While I listened, I also watched; I stood against that wall with the same piss-warm drink, watching how these people danced. They weren't doing the drunken bugaloo like we did at the college bars. And it was none of that hippie acid dancing bullshit like they did at Woodstock. These people here had style and grace.

Where I grew up, the hustle meant one thing, but at Zelda it meant partner dancing, and the way they danced, it was like Ginger Rogers and Fred Astaire with teeth. They took dancing to another level. When the couples got on the floor, everybody got out of their way and let them go. I was mesmerized.

Eventually the couples started peeling off until there was just one couple left: Paul Connelly and his girl, Fran. They were the best of the best. There were no bells and whistles in their dancing; they were just smooth. And the way they moved to the music was like they had ears in their feet.

Then the music changed. You heard a soft guitar and a dude preaching about getting drugs off the streets. Then "Bam," rolling drums and the lyric, "Brothers gonna work it out." It was a single from one of the first Blaxploitation movies ever, "The Mack" performed and written by Willie Hutch.

This song changed the vibe in the room. All of a sudden, a bunch of guys came on the dance floor with no girls, facing each other like a competition. It was like a scene from *West Side Story*, only not as *finoke*. Everybody pulled back so there was a circle, and then one guy jumped in the middle. His name was Ruffy Mugica. He was like Gene Kelly on steroids. We eventually became best of friends and roommates.

When he finished, Ruffy pulled back off the floor into the circle and another guy, T. DeGregorio came out and danced solo. He was different than Ruffy, more animated. He was Gene Kelly meets Fred Astaire and one of the greatest dancers I've ever seen. He was already a legend in the Boston area.

The next guy who jumped in wasn't as good, but you could tell he had the love. People went crazy for him. His name was Benny the Blood. He was a hairdresser at John Dellaria's first salon, which was in Boston on Newbury Street. There, they charged twenty-five dollars for a haircut, when I used to pay two-fifty at Mimmies for a boys' number three. Dellaria's was a whole different world; they asked you if you wanted a cappuccino at the door. The funny thing about Benny was that he was a top-of-the-line hair stylist with the worst rug you ever saw in your life. To make matters worse, the wig was always askew, tilted to the left or tilted to the right. If it had legs, and said "meow," you could name it Fluffy. He eventually became my hairdresser and a pal.

When Benny the Blood was done, another guy jumped in, but nobody knew him. And unless you were known at Zelda, you got five seconds to impress the crowd in the middle of that circle. That was your window. And if you didn't do it, you were out fast.

This guy tonight was no good. Five seconds was up, and some- one shouted: "Yo, fuck face. Get out of here. You can't dance."

Another guy yelled: "Yo, what's wrong with you? Is one leg short- er than the other?"

Another yelled: "What are you an *epilectric*?" Italians never got those big words right.

They didn't have to remove the guy either. He just put his head down and shamefully disappeared into the crowd.

It was the first dance circle I ever saw. In retrospect, the dance circle reflected the grassroots beginning. What was going on in this first-generation Discotheque was organic. It was the true beginning of it all. People took what they knew from growing up as kids and watching those popular musicals and suited it to fit the music. From there, the moves and styles evolved based on what other people did in the moment and on what you saw on the floor. But its roots were in what came before. It was a combination of a Busby Berkeley movie and *Soul Train*. As a blue-collar kid, *Soul Train* always blew me away. But what I saw at Zelda, and at all the good clubs from that era, made *Soul Train* look like Lawrence Welk with a tan.

But there was a problem at Zelda that to me was just so sick. I ran into that thing again that had been pissing me off and baffling me for years, especially since I had been down in Huntsville.

Zelda might have been named after F. Scott Fitzgerald's equally famous wife and glommed off the fame of *The Great Gatsby*, but it was a heavy-duty, hardcore North End, Revere, Charlestown, Southie, East Boston, Italian, and Irish-American club. And all these people were having a great time, dressed to the nines and dancing to R&B music, which was created by black artists, but they wouldn't let brothers and sisters in the club.

Weeks later, I went there and saw something that made me say: "Wow, are you fucking kidding me?" I still feel bad that I didn't at least say something about it at the time, but I wasn't there to be Jesse Jackson.

On that night, there was a black couple in line. They were like Denzel and Halle Berry. He was dressed to perfection, and she was dressed impeccably, without any of that layer cake makeup and sparkles that Italian chicks seemed to think looked good back then. You'd even see them at the beach in full makeup with high heels. But this couple wasn't like that. They were classy. You could tell the guy had money to spend. We were behind them in line. Nobody said anything to them as we moved up. But everybody knew they wouldn't get in. When they got up to the doorman, he didn't even look up. "ID please."

They pulled out their IDs.

"You need another one." By the time he was done, he had ID'd these people three times. And you never got ID'd at that club. For three weeks I had been going, and I never saw that happen. It was obvious what was going on. Zelda had a strict dress code, and being black was outside of it.

When the IDs checked out, the doorman looked them up and down and said: "Your shoelaces."

"What's wrong with my shoelaces?" the guy said.

"They're flat."

"What do you mean?"

"You see mine? They're round. You see his? They're round. You see his? They're round. You can't get in here with flat shoelaces. Do you understand what I'm trying to tell you?"

Everybody else in line was wearing loafers.

The guy looked around. "You're kidding me?"

The doorman stared him down and said, "Do I look like I'm kidding you? Please move out of the way, sir." He had the nerve to call him "sir."

We were right behind this couple. I thought, "Oh my God. I can't believe he just did that."

It just blew my mind that all the music in the club was done by black artists. It wasn't even our music, but they wouldn't even let these people in the club to enjoy it.

The couple walked away with their heads up. After that, I shook my own head, and I walked into Zelda with a new set of eyes. I didn't know that Zelda was like this. Before that moment, to me there were clubs that black people went to and clubs that white people went to in Boston. I just thought that's the way black people wanted it. I didn't realize the white clubs in Boston actually kept them out. It threw me off and made me feel angry. I also felt a little small because I did nothing but watch, and then I edged toward the entrance anyways because I loved the music. Little did I know on that cold winter night standing in line behind the two best-dressed people to never get in the club, someday soon I would help open the doors so people could get in regardless of their shoelaces.

Chapter 5:

YESTERDAY

My friend Carl sat reading the paper. I was asleep on a futon in his place on Commonwealth Avenue. I had no job at the time and was lying around, selling weed and some angel dust just to keep things moving.

Carl gave the paper he was reading a little snap and a shake and said, "Hey. There's a Discotheque called Yesterday auditioning dee-jays—you should go. You're always fucking talking shit about how you could do that. So put your records together and go down there and do it. We'll come down."

"I can do that."

My life revolved around the music at this point. Since I had started going to Zelda, I had tracked down many of the records I'd heard and knew the name of. Back then, discovering new music on your own took effort. It wasn't like there was an internet and you just typed in a term and got what you wanted, or you could download music for free. I had to take scouting missions to the local record stores that had this kind of stuff.

Skippy White's, just around the corner from me in Central Square, Cambridge, was one store that did have the music. One day, I was there pissing and moaning about not being able to find what I wanted when the guy behind the counter told me, "If you want the hardcore R&B and Funk, you should go to our store in Dorchester."

I looked at him and said, "Do I look like I can go to your store in Dorchester?"

The part of Dorchester that he mentioned was hardcore ghetto. It was like the opposite of East Cambridge. White folks just didn't go there. But I took a chance and went. When I stepped into the neighborhood, I was worried about what I might run into, but the worst thing I heard was, "What are you doing here, white boy?"

"I'm going to Skippy White's," I said, and that was it. From that point on, I'd head to Dorchester for the Funk records that Central Square just didn't have. I picked up records like *Nija Walk*, by the Fatback Band; *Put the Music Where Your Mouth Is*, by the Olympic Runners; and Bad Bascombe's *Black Grass*.

By the time the opportunity at Yesterday came around, I had already put together a strong collection. This was the transition period from dive-bar, live-band joints to Discotheques with deejays who were the stars of the room, and I had already taken a master's course in club culture and music by this point. It was time to go legit, and I was ready.

I got dressed to the nines to audition. I wore a *wicked pisser* Nik-Nik shirt and a pair of beige Kork-Ease platform sandals, hit my hair with the vent brush, slid on my lindy-star pinkie ring, took a bath in the hot new cologne, Polo by Ralph Lauren, grabbed a handful of 45s and a bunch of albums, and headed out the door to Yesterday in Kenmore Square. I was familiar with the area because there were a shitload of bars and clubs in Kenmore Square. Fenway Park happened to be there too, and it was surrounded by colleges.

It was also part of a group of clubs known as the Kenmore Club. Downstairs was a place called KKK Katy's. It's where I saw Aerosmith, the J Geils Band, and Boston for the first time. It was a great Rock 'n'

Roll club. And upstairs was a club called Lucifer, which catered to a *made man* and *wise guy* clientele and also had live acts like Harold Melvin and the Blue Notes, the Platters, and blue-eyed soul, pop acts like the Four Seasons. What I didn't know was that Yesterday was down a short alley out back and part of that same complex.

I was surprised it was even there. I walked down the dirty alley and found the entrance. Inside they had a silver dance floor, a deejay booth, and lights, but no Disco ball. This was actually a blue-collar Discotheque and had the sticky floors, shitty furniture, worn out bar stools, and bathroom that smelled like Lysol and piss to prove it. But it was a start. And the location made sense to me. The Kenmore had a rock club downstairs and an exclusive club up. Now they had a Discotheque out back to round it off. Somebody obviously knew what they were doing. I'd find out who he was soon enough.

Inside, I found the rest of the guys who showed for the audition all dressed like shit. They wore Wrangler jeans and khakis, Frye boots, and flannel shirts with unkempt mustaches and beards with long greasy hair. These were Rock 'n' Roll guys, the same kind of guys that would eventually come together behind Steve Dahl for Disco Demolition Night and his *Disco Sucks* campaign because they couldn't dance and didn't like frequent bathing, but that was still like five years away. When I saw them dressed like that, I had to ask myself, "Do they know something I don't know? Is this a Rock 'n' Roll Discotheque?" But if this was a Discotheque like I thought, then I figured that just by the way I looked I would get the job.

It turned out I was right.

The manager's name was Frank Melgar. When he walked in the door, he took a look at the lineup for the audition, then looked at me. He walked over and said: "You guys can leave now. What's *your* name?"

"My name's Joe Carvello."

"What a great fucking name for a deejay: Disco Joe Carvello. What do you have for records, Disco Joe?" I hated that fucking name. But he could have called me Disco Douchebag, and I wouldn't have cared. I wanted to play records for a crowd.

I showed him some of what I'd brought. Then he said: "Great stuff, we have most of them in the booth already. What are these?" And he pointed to a couple of the imports I'd brought. Imports were records that came from overseas. They were limited and rare, and were typically high-energy Disco records; they also often totally sucked. But I knew from going to Zelda that a big thing then were these imports, so I brought a few with me, hoping to impress whoever interviewed me for the job. And I did.

Frank said: "Have you ever deejayed before?"

"I play record hops, but I've never played in a club."

"Here's the deal, you come in tomorrow night around seven o'clock. My co-manager Keith is also the deejay, but I need him to manage full-time, so you're going to take his place. Keith will show you how it's done. He'll tell you what you can and what you can't play. You can bring some records that we don't have in the collection but those are the only records you can leave with at the end of the night. The last deejay who stole records from us can't deejay anymore. You know what I mean?"

I heard him, but my mind was racing. "Wow, this guy's talking like I already have the job."

I left the club practically cartwheeling down the alley. I couldn't wait to tell Carl and the crew that I was going to start deejaying at Yesterday the following night.

As soon as I got home, I told the guys what was up and started making phone calls. I called everybody, focusing on chicks, and begged them to come to the club for my audition night. Nobody knew where or what Yesterday was. When I told them where it was located, they all said: "Really, I didn't even know other Discotheques existed in Boston except for Zelda." I felt that way too, but these clubs were popping up like mushrooms.

"I want to give you a heads up," I said, because I didn't want to mislead them, "This isn't Zelda. It's different. You still can't wear jeans and sneakers, and no t-shirts, but I got a feeling this club has a big college crowd."

Wednesday night came. I dressed basically the same as I had for the interview: nice pair of pants, nice Nik-Nik; but instead of Kork-Ease, I threw on a pair of Giorgio Brutini's. The night's bath was sponsored by Aramis, in lieu of Polo.

Carl gave me a ride. As I got out of the car, he looked at me and said, "Good luck, Cavell." He's the only guy that ever called me that. He still does.

I walked into the club, and Keith Langdon, the Deejay/Co-Manager, walked up to me. Keith was dressed in a lime-green, poly-ester-blend three-piece suit, a pair of green platform shoes with a white ruffled shirt underneath, and vent brushed hair. He looked like the best man at a praying mantis wedding. But he was a drop-dead handsome kid. He gave me a huge smile, shook my hand and said, "My name is Keith; you must be Joe?"

He made me feel super comfortable. "Come up to the booth. Let me show you how this works."

I followed him. The Yesterday deejay booth was on the edge of the dance floor and was elevated by about four feet. Inside, there was also only about four feet of headroom, so you had to sit on a chair to deejay.

I crawled up into the booth with Keith. The chair there had wheels so you could slide back and forth to get the records and not hit your head on the ceiling. There were two turntables facing the floor with volume knobs and, in between the turntables, an amplifier with toggle switch and microphone. Behind me, lined up on the wall were all the 45s and albums they had in their library.

Keith said, "I'll give you a minute to go through them. And, by the way, every two weeks I go out and buy new music to keep us current."

"Do you go to Skippy White's?" I asked eagerly.

"No, I don't. We don't play n****r music here," he said, bursting my bubble in more ways than one. "The last time the owner came through here and the deejay was playing a Funk record, the deejay got fired and I got suspended."

I was wondering how he made the distinction. I thought, "Here we go again with this shit." I felt like I was about to become part of what made me sick the most. I was afraid of that, but I just put it to the back of my mind. I needed to be a deejay. There was no other choice.

Crouching by the back wall of the booth, I shuffled through the records and found everything I hadn't been able to find on my own. Keith was from New York, and whenever he went home, he bought records and brought them back to the club. It made me think that New York had to be incredible. He had all these hard-to-get records like "Something Fishy Is Going On" by Universal Mind; "Sugar Pie Guy" by the Joneses; "Stop I Don't Need No Sympathy" by Lyn Roman; "Half A Cup" by Reggie Garner; "Date With The Rain" by Eddie Kendricks, and hundreds of others.

Then Keith said, "Here's how it works." He went on to explain that the left volume knob was for the left turntable and the right knob for the right. If you had a knob in the off position and put the needle on the record, then you could hear the song through the headphones but not on the speakers. By the way, I was using the club's headphones that night, which was disgusting. I *skeeved* them because only God knows who had put them on before me. I would definitely be going out and buying my own pair the following day. Before I did that, I finished the tutorial on how this thing worked. I had been wondering how Andrew did it all along, so I was all ears and more than happy to have the information.

What you did at that time was cue up one song in the headphones. When you heard it begin, you held the record stationary and, therefore, silent. Once the song on the other turntable, the one playing on the speakers, was about to end, you let go of the record you were holding and turned up that volume while you turned down the volume on the other. For a few seconds, both records played together at different volumes, until the first one faded out. Everybody's heard it done, but it was new then and rare to find someone doing it.

I felt like I was being inducted into a secret fraternity, and this was the handshake. I had already showed him my decoder ring records, and I was dressed for the part.

Eight o'clock rolled around and the only people in the club were a "menza menza" waitress and the bartender. I went up to the booth and played my first record, which was "Shining Star" by Earth, Wind & Fire. But I was playing for an empty club.

I played some more records until eight thirty came around, and still none of my friends were there. Just as I took notice, Keith came up and said, "Where are your friends?"

"Come up for a second. I'll give them a call."

"Just put on a long record," he said.

"Ok." So I put on a song called "Who Is He and What Is He to You" by Creative Source. It was almost twelve minutes long. I went over to the bartender and got change for a dollar: ten dimes. It still only cost a dime to make a phone call then.

The phone booth was by the entrance to the club. There I noticed that the doorman, Greg Lee, was black. And that was strange to me because they had told me I couldn't play Funk, which was considered *black* music, but they had a black guy at the door. It was a strange world. But the reason for it would become evident before too long.

At that point, I started throwing dimes in the phone.

When my friends picked up, I said: "Where the fuck are you?"

Everybody gave the same answer, "We're on our way." Which meant they were guzzling Jack Daniels and doing lines.

"They're coming," I shouted to Keith as I passed him on the dance floor on the way to the booth.

He just gave me a look.

I played a few more records, and then the boys and girls started piling in. They immediately went to the bar, bought drinks, and broke my balls a bit. Soon more folks streamed in, probably regulars, and all of a sudden, I took a breath—we had a little thing going.

Even with the small crowd, the dance floor was empty. I couldn't understand this because I was playing all the records that packed the floor at Zelda, but I was new to this.

Then out of the corner of my eye, I saw this waitress who was a little chubby getting bothered by a group of guys I didn't know. She walked away and quickly came back with the drink order on a tray. Their table was right next to the booth. As she got to the table one of the guys said: "I never seen a fatter waitress." But before he had the chance to say another word, she smashed the metal tray full of beers over his forehead. Blood gushed everywhere. Yesterday didn't have bouncers, so the bartender jumped over the bar. I don't know why because it seemed like the waitress had it under control. As he went over the bar, he screamed, "Greg," who was manning the door. Together they grabbed the guy and threw him and his friends out the back—teamwork. You never saw a waitress from Zelda do that.

That seemed to clear the air. There were more people here now too, but still nobody on the dance floor. I also noticed that some couples came in who looked a little too nice to be there, but they hadn't come in by accident. They stayed a few minutes, and then a guy came from a side door and took them with him. I didn't find out until later that this was a back entrance to Lucifer, and it was the entrance the guys who didn't want to be seen coming in the front door used to get into the club.

While I was watching that, Keith came out of nowhere and said, "You're playing great music, but you're not getting 'em to dance. Get on the microphone and get them out there." The scene felt more embarrassing since my friends weren't even dancing.

As he said that, I got on the microphone and said, "Hi everybody, hope you're having a good time. Come up and dance. Here's Gil Scott-Heron 'The Bottle.'" I figured this was a no-brainer because it was a monster in Zelda. But I got nothing.

At that point, Keith got in the booth and said to me, "Get out of there. Let me show you how it's done."

"What the fuck. Get up off your asses and dance. The first four couples on the floor get a free drink." When he said that a gang of people scampered to the floor.

Keith looked at me at that point and said, "There you go. That's how it's done. Don't abuse the privilege. It's for emergencies only. Now keep them on the floor. We already have salty pretzels. Make them sweat so they want to drink."

After a while, I would put my own spin on that dance floor competition. I'd say something like: "First four guys on the floor will get a blow job from the waitress." That always worked. We never paid up.

I learned how to play two records together and read a crowd real quick that night. When it was over, Keith told me it was the most people they'd had there on a Wednesday night, ever. "People usually use Yesterday to warm up before they go to Katy's or Lucifer," he said. "You kept them here. You got the job. It's fifteen dollars and five beers, or three mixed drinks, a night."

It was official. I was a Disco deejay. Who knew that this night would be the beginning of a forty-year career in the music business? This was now my music, my dance floor, and my family. And I had big plans: I wanted to be the one to light the fuse and make Disco explode, not only in Boston but coast to coast.

CHAPTER 6:

THE BUMP AND THE GODFATHER

In 1975, Disco was about to break, and Yesterday was there to ride the wave.

In just a couple of weeks, my crew came in and took over the club. It was no longer just a stopover bar on the way to Lucifer but a hotspot. We had a whole new audience too. It was like in *The Wizard of Oz* when the movie goes from black and white to color, and I witnessed it from a few feet above the dance floor.

I played Wednesday nights, which conflicted with Zelda's big weeknight. But I didn't worry about being up against the marquee name in Boston; I just focused on the people on the dance floor.

I'd tell people, "Hey, I'm deejaying Wednesdays at Yesterday in the Kenmore, why don't you come down? First drinks on me." I didn't even consider that they would come because Zelda was their home away from home. But as the weeks went by, the people from Zelda did start showing up at Yesterday. I'm talking about those guys and couples whose moves had left me in awe a few months back. And these legends were coming to my club and dancing to my setlist. We really got the Zelda's crowd coming in when we ran a dance contest with a thousand-dollar prize. Zelda held contests too, but they only handed out trophies. And with a thousand dollars at stake, we pulled the best dancers in Boston, like Brian Harkins and Linda Demay—unbelievable. The winner the first night was Ruffy Mugica.

But as well as it went with having the Zelda's crowd come down, it was never so apparent that Yesterday was a dive-bar Disco as when these beautiful, tragically hip people arrived at our door. They didn't mean to be intimidating—that was just something you brought on yourself when you saw them. And though they might have made some of us uncomfortable, they weren't there to judge: the dance floor and the music were the whole reason they came. They sure weren't there for the décor, as the place was still a shithole. It needed to be revamped, which soon happened.

As we started making money, the ownership brought in nicer stools, tables, and chairs. We even got better looking waitresses, which was easy to do, considering the ones we had before were borderline gargoyles. The bartenders weren't allowed to smoke behind the bar anymore either, and they wore tuxedo shirts and bowties.

I'd walked in at the right time: just as it was morphing into a real Discotheque. Not only did the place start looking better, it smelled better. Instead of piss, beer, and cigarettes, you smelled Pantene, Emeraude, and Charlie, which to us was the smell of victory. It was like the ugly girl in grammar school with the braces, pimples, and bad hair, but you meet her five years later and she's Sophia Loren.

And they weren't just drawing beers at the bar—now they were making real drinks. These were Disco drinks: Stingers, Black Russians, Harvey Wallbangers, Sex on the Beaches, Tequila Sunrises. No more pretzels on the bar, no more potato chips. We weren't just serving Bob's Vodka in a can anymore—you could also get Smirnoff. And we upgraded from Martini and Rossi plastic-cork champagne to Moet, but Dom Perignon was still exclusive to Lucifer. They even ditched the foosball tables and brought in backgammon tables. Backgammon was a big early Discotheque thing. There were even fewer fights in the club now.

I couldn't believe how fast the change happened. Then one night, and this was early on, I went upstairs to get paid, which we called "getting an envelope." Greg Lee, the black doorman, was sitting outside of Henry Vara's office talking with Frank's assistant manager. I didn't realize it until I got closer, but the assistant manager was yelling at Greg, and he didn't bother to stop on my account. What he said blew my mind: "There were too many n****rs in here tonight, Greg."

And I'm thinking: "Not this shit again." I had noticed from the booth that there were a few more black people in the audience that night. Typically, at least in my short time there, there were only three regular brothers in the club. There was one regular, who was probably the first guy to dance on my dance floor. He was the king of the bump and was still there until the day I left the club. Another was T.Y. the pimp. He hung in Lucifer, drove a white Lincoln Continental Mark III with gold trim and Zebra interior, and sported a white fur coat all seasons of the year. The last was Freddy Jones. He was a "player" upstairs.

It dawned on me then that it was not an accident that there were only three black guys in the whole Kenmore Club at any given time. And there were never any black chicks at all, which really didn't piss me off as much as bum me out. I had never been with a black chick before, and I knew if a few came in, I'd go home with at least one of them. Those were the perks of being the deejay.

But until that point, I hadn't realized having so many brothers in here was a sin. After all, Greg on the door was black. That just threw me off at first. What I heard in the office made things crystal clear.

"Why do we have you at the door, Greg? Why do we have you on that fucking door?" But he answered his own question. "You keep the n*****s out."

Just then Henry Vara came out of his office, which we were just outside of. He looked pissed, "You know I don't like that word."

Frank's assistant shrank in front of Vara.

"I'll take it from here," Vara said. Then he turned to Greg. "You come in here and see me," and then he pointed to me, "You. You, I'll see you next."

Greg went into Henry's office and left the door open. I could hear everything they said. "Look, I told you a thousand times," Henry began, "I can't have blacks coming down that alley. We're not keeping them out; we're just not letting them in. You'd think they wouldn't want to come down an alley next to a club called KKK Katy's."

Greg just nodded. I could hear Henry laugh a little, "Ok, here's your envelope." And he laughed again.

I heard Greg come back and say, "Thanks, godfather."

How Greg took that shit I don't know, but he was a great guy, and at that club he was family—don't get it twisted. Nobody but our group was allowed to fuck with Greg. We did abuse him, of course, but he was there, and the fact that he was black only widened the net to hit him with shots. He was the perfect target. When Greg walked in, I might say something from the booth like, "Attention Greg Lee, Attention Greg Lee. Kenny McDonough has a flat. He doesn't have a spare. Can he borrow your lips?" People would laugh, and Greg would say something like: "Fuck you, your mother didn't mind these lips last night." He had some great greaseball comebacks. But if anybody fucked with him, or if somebody called him a n*****r, or anything in that zone, then they were put to sleep, a.k.a. knocked the fuck out, and woke up in the dumpster in the alley.

Aside from joking around sometimes, I wasn't into this segregated bullshit. I didn't like it. If I did, I'd have stayed in East Cambridge. But right then I didn't see anything I could do about it. I couldn't just kick a redneck in the face, like in Huntsville, and change the way the club worked. So I acquiesced to how it was and made up my mind to do what I could as the opportunity presented itself to me.

Things were heating up fast, though. Vara might have allowed some segregation, but he was no dummy. He saw what was happening and how the currents were shifting. In other words, he knew how much money Yesterday brought in before me, and how much it brought in on the Wednesday nights after me. And it wasn't just Wednesdays anymore. After a couple weeks in the club, I was working Friday and Saturday nights as well. Now the club made big money. A club can't exist with weekend nights alone, and I was giving Vara such a big, over-the-top Wednesday night that he made his nut in one weeknight. The people danced nonstop to the point where the bartenders would throw ice cubes at me to get me to play a slow song so that people would come off the dance floor and buy drinks.

It was only natural that I became a deejay, the most logical reason being that I had a vowel at the end of my name, and the crowds were made up of mostly Italian and Irish. I was half mick too, and I was also accessible and straight, and I got it. I didn't pull any attitude on people when they came up to the booth, which made them feel like they were part of what was going on, not an outsider.

There were several other deejays in Boston at that point, two of which worked on my off nights. A few just played records in clubs with no personality, and the rest were almost exclusively and profoundly gay, and they had 100% gay audiences that were so gay their dogs were gay—their furniture was gay.

My goal wasn't to be any one thing but to get as many people in that room as I could and keep them coming back. If that meant taking requests, then I tried to accommodate. But every once in awhile, I'd get a guy who would demand a request or constantly badger me until I played the record. If he got real aggressive, I'd come out of the booth, and, before he could react, he'd be doing the horizontal bump on the dance floor. And trust me, that wasn't pretty.

I knew my audience and what records the regulars wanted to hear when they showed up. I'd announce them when they came in. "Ladies and gentlemen, one of my best friends, Ricky Maciejko, is here, and he's packing a trout." Ricky was and still is my oldest and dearest friend.

I also put together a weekly playlist of the twenty hottest songs from the week before, along with four or five of the new records I was playing. At first, I paid the cost of Xeroxing the list myself, but after the management saw everybody walking out with a copy, they decided to charge for it. Then I got motivated and picked up local advertisers to make a couple extra bucks, which turned out well for me when the owner of Webb's, Morris Fine, gave me a pair of tickets to the sixth game of the 1975 World Series: Reds versus Red Sox at Fenway Park—one of the greatest games of all time.

I started making that list at first because the audience couldn't pronounce half the song titles and musicians' names. They always had their own spin: "Hey, Joey, would you play 'Date with Loraine.'" When they meant "Date with the Rain" by Eddie Kendricks. Or, "Joey, will you play something by Kool in the Gang?" When it was Kool *and* the Gang. Or after 1976, when the synthesizer sound got big, someone would say: "Yo, Joey, will you play that record with the *sympathizers*," instead of synthesizers. Every record had synthesizers then.

And God forbid you didn't play one of these *greasettes* requests. It was always one of those wiseass Italian chicks who aggressively made requests. One night, I'd already played the record this girl was asking for. "I played that 20 minutes ago," I said. At which point she threw a drink in my face. And when the ice cubes were still spinning on the record, she looked at me and said: "You're a sucky *deejays* anyways." She added the S to "deejay," which was another Italian thing.

Regardless of what happened, though, you always played the mob guys, wiseguys, and coke dealers requests in a timely fashion. Typically, if I saw a mob guy come up for a request, I had the song he was looking for narrowed down. For a while, nine out of ten times he asked for "Fly Robin Fly," by Silver Convention. I ended up playing that song four or five times a night.

As we started to pull an audience and we were no longer at the bottom of the list in Boston nightlife, we started getting characters in the club. It meant we were doing something right. Even Oscar the Flower Guy, who sold roses for a dollar exclusively at Zelda and Lucifer, started coming to Yesterday.

People also began coming to the club strictly for the music, which was starting to drive the lifestyle, where the lifestyle once drove the music. Early on, I might've had one or two people come up to ask what I was playing; now I'd get fifteen or twenty in the same night who cared what we played. People were also accepting new music easier.

The Discotheque was changing the way people discovered records, and I was putting them onto it.

People were bored to death of the Debby Boones and the Anne Murrays on Top 40 Radio. Listening to that music, you wanted to open a fucking vein. But we had all these high-energy pop and R&B records that you just couldn't get anywhere else. And that's what people were coming for. Then they started coming not just to hear records they liked but to find records they were going to like. I loved being the one to bring them in. I couldn't even believe they were paying me to do this. It used to be that radio was where you got your music from, but not anymore. And not only that, I never knew what radio deejays looked like, but these people knew who I was.

Discotheques became an event, like concerts were. But with the Discotheque, you didn't have to worry about missing out when the band moved to the next city or seeing the band twice and repeating the same show. The music was there every night, and there was always a new song or two. The music was always familiar but always fresh.

Now that Discotheques were starting to draw all these newcomers out, you could see and feel the revolution coming together. If new people walked into Yesterday wearing clothes that showed they were out of place and belonged maybe in another club, we didn't shun them—we wanted to flip them. What I loved to see were people with mundane jobs coming to this club and becoming somebody else. It was the music that separated them from their miserable daytime existences. And that was Disco. A garbage man during the day was a star out there on the floor at night, and no one cared. I had guys who danced for four or five hours straight by themselves. They were getting their exercise in that club. Some girls were chubby when they first started coming in, and then all of a sudden after a month you'd look out on the dance floor and they'd lost the weight and were looking good. They dressed better too, got rid of the mustache, slapped on some makeup, and finally had the looks to get laid.

Despite that enthusiasm, it was still difficult to get new stuff to go over. Sometimes halfway through playing a new song, people would come out on the dance floor, but most of the time they'd give me a *bagetha*. Eventually, if I had a song that I thought would be a hit, I'd play it two or three times a night. After a while, it would become one of their favorite songs. That's how we got Donna Summer's "Love to Love You Baby" to go over. We loved the record, and she was from Boston. We knew it was going to be a big hit, but we just couldn't get it to stick. All the deejays had this experience, but there was a consensus and solidarity among us that we loved this record, and so we stuck by it. And that solidarity proved that the Disco deejay had the power to move the music dial. It took six to eight weeks before finally it went over and became, from where I sit, the most important record of the Disco revolution because it broke arguably one of the greatest female artists of all time, Donna Summer, wide open. That song was ours, and she was ours, and with that victory we knew what was coming.

CHAPTER 7:

RORER 714

Every Wednesday, Friday, and Saturday night, Yesterday was on *fire*. There were times the crowd would become so frenzied, the music so magnificently loud and thunderous, that I would get emotional. The hot-blooded feedback that emanated out of the crowd and just the innate love of the music would sometimes become overwhelming. Never in my life had I witnessed such raw excitement. It wasn't like this at Zelda. Because Zelda was a scene—here it was a family, and people knew it the second they walked in.

People were usually out of their minds and sweating by the end of the night. Last call for alcohol was always wild: "You don't have to go home, but you can't stay here!" I'd roar over the mic.

"No! One more, Joe, one more!"

If I played one more song and Vara caught me, he'd flip out: "What the fuck are you doing playing music past 2:00 AM? We could lose our fucking license! You should fucking know better. What the fuck, turn it off NOW!"

But when he got to the register and saw the take, he'd back off. After that, he'd let me get away with it every now and again. The take from week to week had jumped so much that we leveled it off at a certain number, and everything above that number was ours. At the end of the night, the full-time employees would get a little "taste." Back in those days, all the club owners knew they were going to get *ganked*, but you didn't abuse the privilege. There was a difference between stealing and skimming.

One example of this was the way we ran the Something for Nothing Nights. We'd give out gift certificates to a local pizza place or to Webb's clothing store to get people in and charge a two-dollar cover. At the end of the night, someone would win the raffle prize based on the take at the door, which would be about a hundred and fifty or two hundred dollars. Of course we rigged the raffle. The doorman would give me the winning ticket, and I'd tear it in half and give it to whoever I chose, or whoever we decided. One night the winner was my cousin, Jimmy Jim. But whoever won, we always squared up down the street at the Aegean Fare restaurant—more than just raffle tickets got settled at that place.

I can still see Lupo out front—he had written his number with a magic marker on a piece of pita bread and handed it to a girl. "Call me," he said, "and if you don't call me, you can eat me."

Working at the club the way I was, I got to know everybody. Then one night a guy came through Yesterday on his way to Lucifer. Harold Melvin and the Blue Notes were playing. It turned out that this guy was already an R&B music legend in the Boston area. He was a white guy who knew more about R&B than anybody, no matter what color they were. He probably had one of the biggest R&B record collections in the world. He was a music freak, like I was, only he knew way more than I did. His name was Eddie B. He was from Charlestown, a tiny city in Boston teeming with Irish pride. Those "Townies" listened to Motown 24/7 but wouldn't have the Temptations over for Thanksgiving. Yet even though he was from Charlestown, Eddie B. wasn't a racist—for as many people in Charlestown that were racist, there were more that weren't; it just happens that the empty barrels make the most noise.

Eddie B. worked in the printing shop at Mass General Hospital and also sold the hard-to-find records. At night, he roamed the Boston club scene. When Martin Luther King Jr. was assassinated, James Brown performed the next night at the Boston Garden. The only white guy who had the nuts to go to that show was Eddie B. It's said that James Brown saved Boston, albeit temporarily, when he and the mayor, Kevin White, under advisement of a black city councilman, Tom Atkins, made the risky decision to let the show go on. The city also decided to air the concert live on TV, which kept a lot of people indoors and off the streets. The mayor walked on stage that night with Mr. Dynamite and rallied for peace to the crowd while the Boston police stood on the sidelines itching to use their batons. They never got the chance. Kevin White and James Brown kept that room and everyone's heads cool that night, while the rest of America burned.

I noticed Eddie B. when he came in the room that night. My booth was like a watchtower where I saw everything develop. When someone was going to the bathroom to do blow, I'd make noise over the speakers and then give them the "what about the deejay?" look when they turned to me. Most people knew what the bathrooms were actually for and how to stay breezy about it. You didn't "snort" in the bathroom, you sniffed. Coke etiquette exists.

But in the booth that night I noticed a white guy standing midway in the room with his arms crossed, watching me. I put on "Beware of the Stranger" by the Hypnotics. His eyebrows went up, and he came over and introduced himself. The first thing he said was, "That's a great record. I don't hear that a lot. My name is Eddie B."

He was just there a few minutes, but in that time he told me about another deejay I should check out. He said his name was John Luongo—a white guy who played at an all-black club called the Rhinoceros in Boston's financial district.

"I'm really good friends with John. You should meet him. I think you guys would hit it off. Besides that, the guy's a great deejay. Nobody plays shit like this guy plays."

I gave Eddie B. my mother's number. You always gave out your mother's number then. Besides that, ninety percent of us still lived with our moms. I told him to call me and we'd go to the Rhino together to meet John Luongo.

"They call him TC—top cat," Eddie said, and then, "I'm going next door to see Teddy, maybe I'll come later." Teddy Pendergrass, lead singer of Harold Melvin and the Blue Notes, was playing next door. Little did I know that this first night with Eddie B. was the beginning of a lifelong friendship. Eddie B. and I are like brothers. I've owed him twelve hundred bucks for records for like a hundred years. And as I told Eddie B., I'd rather owe it to you than cheat you out of it.

I wrote down TC's name on a piece of paper along with Eddie B.'s. I had to write it down because I knew by the end of that night I'd be so fucked up I'd hardly remember my own name, especially since Gustavo, the Argentinian bartender, had brought enough Quaaludes for everybody. It was hard to miss that stamp: RORER 714. Ludes, or "disco biscuits" as we affectionately called them, were a muscle relaxant that induced euphoria. They sent tingles through your whole body and relaxed everything so intensely that you'd be a walking noodle and fall in love with everybody. It was like a love pill. If you got too speedy on coke and didn't want to drink anymore but wanted to come down, you could take a Quaalude or a Seconal or Tuinal to find the combination of downs, liquor, and blow to even you out.

After those drugs came crystal meth, which was the bad shit. It was the poor man's blow. It cost sixty bucks for half a gram of blow and thirty bucks for half a gram of crystal meth. We nicknamed it "catpiss" because it smelled like it and burned hot. Unlike coke, which would give you a good high and then combined with downs you could fall asleep, the only way down from crystal meth was a bottle of Nyquil.

As that night picked up after Eddie B. walked out, I could hardly even talk in words. I could still spin records though. And that's what I did. I put on a long song and took a bathroom break, which meant I had to go do some zip-a-dee-doo-dah. After the bathroom, I zipped over to the bar and was so fucked up that I *merred*. That meant the cocaine had given me jaw hockey: my jaw couldn't stop moving from left to right.

When I *merred* at the bar, I gave up talking altogether and pointed to the vodka and then pointed to the cranberry. The bartender made me a drink, and from that point on we began developing a system. Soon I'd hold up one finger for an Absolut and cran, and two for a shot of tequila with an Absolut and cranberry back. This way I could avoid talking when I was too incoherent to verbalize anything. I didn't like asking the waitresses to get my drinks because it pulled them away from paying customers.

I returned to the booth and climbed up and in with my drink in my hand. I sat down and pushed myself around on the office chair. One kick sent me to the wall where I grabbed another record to be ready when the song ended. I was pretty skeed from the blow. The shit was obviously a little speedy to say the least because when I pushed off the back wall, I pushed too hard and launched out of the booth. As I flew out, I gripped the arms as if that could save me. I was fucked.

Everything went silent. As I came down, I looked at the crowd who was looking back at me. I saw their eyes widen and their mouths drop. But I landed on all four wheels, and a sigh of relief went up as they watched me roll by. If I had to translate, they were thinking: "Holy shit. That crazy bastard stuck the landing." Then they started to cheer and shout: "Joe! Joe! Joe!"

With that, I raised my hand like I was the Queen of England and winked at the crowd. But the chair kept rolling, and the back door was open, and I went right out the door and tumbled down the twelve steel alley steps. All I could hear were the screams from the people inside; some were laughs, others were screams of horror. I'm sure there were some assholes up there who said, "Fuck him. Hey baby, what's your sign?"

I was so high that despite the tumbling, bouncing, and the ending crash on the pavement, I didn't feel any pain. I just got off the ground, grabbed the chair, dragged it up the stairs, and ran to the booth because I had to make the mix. I was bloody and bruised and almost out on my feet, but I didn't want any dead air. I had already lost the dance floor; they were all looking at me. But I had to at least keep the music going.

Someone came up and asked if I was all right. So I started to take stock of the situation. My first question was, "How's my hair?"

"Fine."

"Then I'm alright. Fuck! That was a buzz kill. Would you grab me a drink and a lude?"

I started looking at myself at that point: bloody pants, bumps, and bruises. I was pissed off most of all about my scuffed shoes. But my left arm was far more black-and-blue than all the other bumps and bruises I had. Later, when I sobered up, I noticed my left arm was clicking. At the hospital, they told me it was fractured, but I finished the night. THAT'S DISCO.

Chapter 8:

SHELLY, JUMBO, CIGARS & RAZZABONES

As time passed and the club became more and more presentable, I was getting into a groove of my own and becoming more recognizable and respected as a Disco deejay. The lifestyle was crazy, but I was young and in love with it. I could handle the late, late nights and all the action that went along with it. My friends were always in and out, and the atmosphere was nothing short of love and family.

And then my first and future ex-wife, Shelly, walked into the club. She lived almost across the street from the Kenmore but, like a lot of people, never knew we were there. She had been drawn into the Disco scene the same way I had been and had been through the same experience at Zelda that I had, where the first night she walked into that club it blew her mind. When she found Disco, she was in her element.

She was from Rhode Island originally, but after graduating college, she stayed in Boston. Now she was in my club and was about to become a regular. Later on, she told me she almost didn't make it to the club that night at all. She met some maniac in the alley who gathered her into a bear hug and invited her to a party the following night. I know who it was, too. It was Carl Lupo, AKA Carl Lafong. He was like my brother.

There wasn't much that escaped my attention from the deejay booth, but I didn't notice Shelly when she first walked in. It wasn't until later when Carl pointed her out that I saw her. Carl jumped up into the booth smiling like he had something important to tell me. I instinctively protected my turntable. I can't count the number of times Carl ran the needle across one of my records. He'd climb in the booth and start reaching for shit that wasn't his or pointing out onto the floor. But no matter what, Carl and I were like brothers. Now he was pointing at her and talking so loudly that I was sure she could hear every word he said. Much later, she admitted she did. He let me know he invited her to Frankie D.'s party the following night, and then he jumped out of the booth as fast as he had come and disappeared into the crowd.

I didn't pay much more attention to the girl he had just pointed out. He was showing me girls all the time, and it was seldom that I spent the rest of the night fixated on the one he showed me. And besides, I had more on my plate that night.

We had some guys in the house that night who were the most suspicious looking motherfuckers I'd ever seen—so shifty and strange. I watched them like a hawk, and none of them would look me in the eye. They had been there before, too. It was clear they enjoyed the music, spent money, and sometimes brought girls, but they were different and out of place, and that made me take notice whenever they arrived. That night I caught one of them pickpocketing a girl on the floor, practically in front of me. He took her wallet out of her pocketbook. He was so slick I practically missed it, even though I was looking right at him.

She was none the wiser, but when I saw it, I jumped down and grabbed him by the shirt before he could hand her wallet off to someone else. That's how they do it; it's like a bucket brigade. I dragged him to the back door and launched him down the stairs so hard he landed on the bottom two steps and the pavement. That was it for him.

His friends immediately came up to me. At first, I thought they wanted a problem, and I was ready to give it to them. But the guy who was obviously in charge stepped up and said, "Listen, we're sorry."

"You didn't do anything. Your friend did."

"We're Gypsies," he said, "We do everything together."

And I thought, "*That's* what they are." I knew there was something different about those guys.

"Again, we're sorry. We'll make sure our people never do that again or anybody else does either."

"How you going to do that?" I asked.

"We can smell thievery. We'll help you."

Now this seemed suspicious. "Why do you want to help me?"

"We love the club and love the music you play; we want to stay here."

After that, we let the guy who stole back into the club. And the guy who spoke for them, it turned out his name was Nicky. Of course, once we found out his name was Nicky, he became Nicky the Gypsy.

They were in the club all the time and became part of the circle, and some of them even felt comfortable enough to come to the booth and ask that I play specific records or ask me what I had just played. One day, I didn't have the time to answer when one of them asked me for the name. Instead, I just handed him the record and turned back to what I was doing. A few nights later, he walked up to the booth again and asked me to play the record with the yellow label. I realized then that he couldn't read. They never went to school— at least the group I was dealing with didn't. Instead, they were home schooled in thievery, scamming, aluminum siding, and palm reading, but not literacy. I had an idea that they kept them illiterate to keep them on the hustle. But despite that, there was a certain romance to being a Gypsy.

I developed an affinity for the group: their way of life, their secret weirdo codes, and the way they dressed. I became close with some of them, especially Kiki. She died of an overdose not long after. Her funeral procession to the Mount Auburn Cemetery in Watertown was immense, filled with panic and confusion. At the cemetery one of the Gypsies lifted the lid to Kiki's casket. I saw that inside they had stashed enough drugs to fuel the club for a week as gifts to send her on her way.

The night of the Gypsy King was also the night my father came to the club for the first time. I had been trying to get him to come over since I got the gig. Then, all of a sudden, he just showed up with his friends Beppo, Saipan, and Zoro. Growing up in the neighborhood, everybody had a nickname. Lots of guys had two, but there was only one guy that I knew who had three: my dad. They called him Jumbo, because he had been a small baby; Cigars, because he was dark like a cigar; and Razzabones because, as he grew up, he was as skinny as a rail. The name that was most popular was Jumbo, which Italians pronounced *Chumbo*.

When I saw him across the way, I almost started to cry—I was so damned happy and shocked. I had been a bad kid; I mean really bad. He threw me out of the house when I was eighteen, and that was after I got thrown out of the army. I had thrown a huge drug-fueled party at home when my parents were gone. My Uncle Tony came to try and break it up. We came to blows, and I almost broke him up. After that, well, things became a little difficult between father and son.

He was standing at the bar watching me as I got on the mic and yelled, "Ladies and gentlemen, my dad is here with Beppo, Saipan, and Zoro. Dad, drinks are on me. Seven and 7s please—keep 'em coming!" I had just put on "Fly Robin Fly" too, which would become one of his favorite songs. Wise guys loved that song.

A friend took over for me, and I went down to the bar. As I got close, I saw the bartender serving up the drinks I had ordered from the booth. I broke my usual drinking pattern and had a Seven and 7 with him; that was Seagram's Seven mixed with 7 Up.

Then Beppo looked around and said, "I like this song. It's a great song. I love this song. What's it called?"

"Fly Robin Fly," I said with the straightest face I could manage. How the fuck couldn't you know the name of that song when it's the only lyric?

My father just patted me on the shoulder. I could tell he was proud. After that, he started coming in maybe three nights a month or more. He got his buzz on in Yesterday and then went on to Lucifer. As it turned out, he knew a lot of guys there. And even though he liked to drink, I never saw him drunk. At my grandmother's house on Sundays, they'd hand him a Coffee Royal when he walked in, which I thought was a fancy coffee, until I took a swig and realized it was whisky.

He was a hard worker from start to finish, though—he'd do ten and twelve-hour days of manual labor, but that guy loved to party, and I was just like him.

When he finally met Shelly, he said to me, "Don't fuck with this girl, I like her." She was a mess when he passed away in '76.

In spite of our rough beginnings and all the fights and evictions, my dad and I finally came full circle.

The following night, Carl and I went to Frankie D.'s house for the party. One thing about Frankie's parties was that he never called them parties. He referred to them as "extravaganzas" instead. They always started off slow, but by the end of the night they would look like Caligula's birthday.

That night, Shelly showed up on her pseudo-date with Carl and brought a gorgeous blond, prom queen type named Dianne along. Dianne literally had the best ass I'd ever seen, and Carl, being the fucking huge asshole he was, jumped all over Dianne and acted like Shelly wasn't even there.

Carl saved himself at the end of the night by inviting himself back to Shelly's apartment by telling her he was going to bring the deejay from Yesterday. "He's my best friend," he added. "His name is Joe, and you're going to love him."

After we left Frankie's, Carl and I followed Shelly and Dianne back to her apartment in Kenmore Square. As always, we were in rare form. Carl was knocking shit over, as usual. Shelly and Dianne were two spectators in their own home, and every once in a while, they moved swiftly enough to save a vase or a lamp or some other knickknack from crashing to the floor. Every fifteen minutes I muttered, "Fucking Carl," as he bumped into her countertops or banged into Dianne. They thought it was funny but were also a little curious about what was wrong with him.

It worked out well for me because I appeared together and with it by comparison. I was the picture of sobriety. More often than not, even when inebriated I often presented as slightly normal, which explains why I was usually the designated drunk driver for our crew. I don't know how I pulled it off, but I usually got everybody home unharmed without dents or pedestrians on the grill of my car.

When the girls went outside to the balcony and left us on our own, we hit up their cabinets for something to eat. We were hungry because we had just puffed some *skunk*. They walked in and Carl was rummaging her freezer. I was eating out of a box of cereal. The night was basically over by that point. But when we left, Carl didn't disappoint—he used his famous sneak attack move on Shelly. There was nothing she could do about it. Shelly wasn't pissed off. I think she knew that Carl was going to be her friend. Everyone needs a friend they can count on for sick and twisted fun. They became really close, like brother and sister. And as for Shelly and me, we just clicked.

Shelly and I were the original Disco couple: we met at a Disco, we did everything at a Disco—our wedding was 100% Disco. She was my other half. And because I was basically a little kid who was all over the place, she would scold me and clean up my mess. We were Disco's adaptation of Wendy and Peter Pan. There is no doubt that I wouldn't be where I am today if it weren't for Shelly. And if there was ever a Jew broad that could be canonized into sainthood, it would be Shelly. Everybody loves her. I'll always love her.

Years later, she'd say she knew I led a double life: "I know you fucked every girl in Boston."

"No, I didn't. I missed two or three."

Chapter 9:

THE RHINO

By now Eddie B. and I had become friendly. He'd stop by the club to shoot the shit and talk music. One night, he asked again if I'd checked out the deejay, John Luongo, at The Rhinoceros Club like he had suggested. I hadn't. Luongo's was a name I had never heard until Eddie B. came into my club. And since Eddie knew everything there was to know about music, I decided I should take his advice and check out the scene. I knew that it was an all-black club. But with my history of trekking all over Dorchester to pick up records, I wasn't that worried about the venue.

I dressed to the nines for my big night out. Eddie couldn't make it that night, so I was flying solo. I went out dressed in my sharp platform sandals, white jeans, white Nik-Nik shirt, wide open to the navel, and a white Jean jacket with white sunglasses. I finished it off with a Pino Sylvestri Cologne bath. You couldn't miss me, and if you did, you sure could smell me. It didn't occur to me until later that I was walking into this joint looking exactly like Casper the Friendly Ghost. The slang for white people at the time was *Casper*. Another was *Honky*, a term brought over from West Africa meaning "red-eared person," which is exactly what would happen to a white lazy-ass slave owner once he stepped out into the sun. The more modern belief is that we remind black people of the white *Drake's Cakes* duck. I don't like that one.

I left my apartment headed for the Rhino. The financial district is basically a bunch of alleys, small tight streets, and one ways. After five p.m. it was a ghost town, but not where I was going. As I turned the corner in the direction of the club, I accidentally bumped into a dude just standing there. This was the end of the line, which snaked three quarters of the way down the block to the doors of the Rhino. No one seemed to notice me at first in the back of the line, but as people queued up behind me, I heard some mumbling in my general direction.

As I got closer to the club, the doorman noticed me. He walked over and stopped, looking me up and down, and then he looked me straight in the eye and said, "Are you sure you're at the right place?" and pointed to the line. "You do know this is a black club?"

"I'm not white. I'm Italian," I said. "There's a big difference." I wasn't even being a smart ass. The doorman let a smirk escape from the corner of his mouth, but aside from that he didn't look amused. Then I added, "I'm here to see John Luongo, he invited me."

The bouncer kept the same expression. He thought for a moment and said, "Alright, if you're okay with TC, then you're okay. Come on in." With that, he grabbed me out of line and brought me through the doors, no cover.

When I entered the room, I may as well have scratched the record. Everyone turned to look. It was like when the crowd does the wave at Fenway Park, the way all those black faces turned in series to see the tall, skinny, all-white, white boy walk in. And this place was jammed to the ceilings. I was starting to second guess my decision to come here. I wasn't even sure if a white guy actually could play this club. And half of the stuff he was playing I didn't even know, including the first song I heard as I came in the door: "Just a Little Bit of

You" one of Michael Jackson's first solo singles. To this day, I play that record every time I spin and remember that moment.

I knew it was MJ right away, but the looks I was getting were throwing me off. I just put my head down and kept on walking. I didn't make eye contact with anybody. With all eyes on me, it seemed like it took a lifetime to make my way over to the stairs to get to the second floor where John had his booth.

When I got to the top of the stairs, I saw it. It was elevated and surrounded on three sides by Plexiglas. As I approached the booth, John put on a record that always reminds me of him, especially what he was doing to it. It was a song by Parliament-Funkadelic "Shit Goddam Get Off Your Ass and Jam." John had two copies of the record and just kept on running the hook from one record to another making a two-minute track basically endless. The place was going absolutely insane.

John's audience looked like Soul Train in a suit. Everybody in that club looked so good, stylish, and swanky. Once I got past the obvious, the Rhino was a lot like Zelda, but here Dakar was the choice of cologne, and I saw only couples dancing—no guys freestyling by themselves. And it seemed like there was an equal number of women and men, so it wasn't a pick-up joint. This was where all the badass black people in Boston went to be comfortable, get great service, and listen to the best music a Boston discotheque had to offer.

As I got close to the booth, I noticed there was one old black guy standing beside it wearing a necklace with a huge bull's head on it, and behind him, leaning up against the wall, was a Louisville Slugger. John's security. I later learned the guy's name was Doc Porter. He loved John. He later became a semi-regular at Yesterday and would come by to see me. He was a great guy, but you didn't fuck with him. One night a guy in front of the booth pointed up and said: "Who's telling the white boy what to play?"

Doc responded, "Motherfucker, that white boy knows more about the music than you and all your nappy-headed pricks put together." He obviously gave Doc some back talk because the next thing you knew the guy was up off the floor like he was wired to the ceiling. As usual, out the backdoor he went. Doc didn't go for any racial shit. It was all about the music and whether you were cool or not. The club was all black, but that's not what it was all about.

I didn't know any of this that first night. I kept looking at Doc, wondering what he would do if I went up to John. I'm sure he noticed me. Everybody noticed me. It took me several minutes to work up the nerve to approach near to the booth. As I got closer, Doc just watched me, which is different than looking at somebody, but he must have guessed I was there to see John. Why else would a white dude, dressed like Elton John, be standing there staring at the booth?

I got my chance to talk to John when he played the next song, which I knew was six minutes long. As soon as I heard it, I went up and introduced myself, "John, I'm Joe Carvello—Eddie B. sent me to see you, and he wasn't bullshitting me when he told me you were the best—I'm the deejay from Yesterday." I said it all together, breathlessly.

I felt nervous as he looked me over, taking in what I had said. "I heard of you," he said. Good old Eddie B. had told him. I breathed normally then and relaxed a little bit. "Eddie said, 'You gotta meet this Carvello kid. He plays like a motherfucker.'"

John was the kind of guy who liked to help out other deejays. After some small talk and number exchanging, he introduced me to the whole club on the mic: "This is Joey, he's an up-and-coming deejay. He plays at Yesterday in Kenmore Square." My first thought was that if this room showed up at Yesterday, I was fucked, and Greg would be out of a job. The whole joint just looked at me, a few nodded, but then it was on. The crowd loosened up with Casper the

Greaseball, and they weren't shy. People were starting to come up and introduce themselves.

John just kept spinning records, keeping people out on the floor, which gave us time to talk. He had an interesting story with a lot of overlap to mine. He had worked as a deejay at a Discotheque called the Townehouse, above the Bull & Finch Pub, which was the bar everyone later knew as *Cheers*. But before that it was just another nightspot trying to make a dollar. He got the gig almost by accident when he was still a student at Northeastern.

John went into the Townehouse with some friends one night. The bar was in a judge's old chamber on the second story, and at the top of the staircase he saw a deejay mixing records live. John approached the deejay, and after they talked a while, John wrote his phone number on a matchbook and said, "If you ever need somebody to fill in, give me a call."

A week later, the owners called him up. The deejay had quit and left them John's number as a referral. Of course he said, "Yes." Like me, he was in the right place at the right time and was willing to take a chance but had no clue what he was doing. He ran down to Everett Music on Norwood Street in Everett and put together a record collection as fast as he could, and then he went into the club early and figured out how to work the sound system. He knew how he should play the records in theory. But the way the system was set up at the Townehouse, he had no idea how to start a record on the heels of another. It sounded like a train wreck when he did it. So he improvised and soon figured out that if he started one record over the other and let it spin until he heard the first note, then pulled it back, there would only be a quick noise over the sound system, and no one would know what it was. Then he could hold the record right there and let it go when the right time came, which would come to be known as a quick cut. This was like how I started out over at

Yesterday but a little more difficult. I guess we were all flying by the seats of our pants. But John was already a well-known veteran before I played my first record.

John quickly became the dance master at the Townehouse, and soon the place was packed with high-energy people. Its proximity to several really cool colleges also helped grow an audience; nearby were Chamberlin Junior College and Emerson. The owners were happy to have the immense crowds, but while those crowds were dancing, they weren't drinking as much as ownership thought they should be, and so they asked John to slow the music down at times to get people off the floor and over to the bar. They suggested he play "Brandy" by Looking Glass, which is one of the greatest pop records of all time, but not even close to a Disco record.

John didn't want to change anything he was doing because he knew it was working, and he especially didn't want to take people off the dance floor when he had worked so hard to get them on it in the first place. But ownership told him that if he didn't slow it down then they would fire him.

"Are you out of your mind?" he said. "I broke my ass to get these people to dance. I'm not going to empty the floor."

He quit, gave them a "go fuck your sister," and went out looking for another gig where he would be better appreciated. At that time, the Rhinoceros was a white businessman's club with a small clientele in the Financial District.

John went into the Rhino, and they gave him the job. They let him play the music he liked and that he wanted to play, which helped turn that club into the number one black club in New England. John had people coming not only from Boston but from Rhode Island and Connecticut and staying overnight just to see and hear him play.

I became a fan immediately, and not just of the music he played—that was a given—but of his mastery of programming and mixing, and of how he read and kept a floor; he was one of the greatest deejays of all time. In return, people would dance to anything John played. He was one of the few who could get away with playing something new, and the crowd would trust him. He would know before the record was even halfway through if it wasn't working because he could read everyone's body language. And even if it didn't go over, he wouldn't lose the floor like would happen at other clubs. The result was that he brought the house down every night on a system that was even worse than what he had used at the Townhouse. It didn't take me long to love and respect this guy like an older brother. He was my mentor and, on occasion, my bail bondsman.

As we sat talking, I saw a devilish look in his eye. "Have you been to the third floor?" he asked.

"I didn't know there was a third floor."

"Not many do." He turned to Doc and said, "Doc, take him up to the third floor."

Doc smiled. "Come on, Elton John." I followed him, and after a few steps he stopped and said, "Not a lot of John's people come to see him, and none of 'em have gone to the third floor. If you have any trouble, just see me."

"I've hardly ever been more comfortable," I responded, and it was the truth. The people here seemed like they knew how to have a good time and still be warm and relaxed. I was never comfortable outside of the city. In a suburban club, if you accidentally bumped into a wired-up grease ball, you were automatically in a fistfight, but at the Rhino you'd just say excuse me and move on.

I thought, "I can't wait to come back here and bring Shelly and a couple of the guys." John had a lot of fans, but almost none of them would go see him at the Rhino. I would go in there and everyone knew who I was, but for me it was all about the third floor.

Doc opened this door that led to a tight staircase, and as soon as he opened it you could smell the weed. John's music was pumping up there as well. We walked in, and it was like heaven. Pimps and hoes, and titties and lap dances. There was coke, weed, and bottles being popped, but not for show. It was for the moment—not the moment itself. People today pop bottles to create a moment. We did it to appreciate one.

I walked in cold, ahead of Doc. When the door opened, everyone turned and did a double take. But then Doc came through the door. All he did was put his hand on my shoulder. That made me feel comfortable.

From that point on, I preferred the third floor at the Rhino. And since then, whenever John and I would be in a funky place, we'd just look at each other. One of us would always say, "It ain't the third floor." Eventually it became my Cheers, where everybody knew my name. I'd walk right past John every night: "Hey John, how you doing? You sound great." He'd give me a nod and a wink.

John also had a radio show with WTBS at MIT, and eventually Ted Turner bought those call letters. John even brought me in and interviewed me. Strangely, I had been to his studio before. It was right behind East Cambridge, and I used to play tennis on the courts which were right above it. For several months, I played above where he spun records, and every time we lost a ball over the fence, it bounced down the flight of stairs that led to where he was. Little did I know that if I had just walked in that front door and gone left, I would have walked into the studio where the first Disco radio show was being broadcast.

To me it was meant to be: kismet.

John's show was called *The Right Track,* and the theme song came from "We're on the Right Track" by Ultra High Frequency of Philadelphia. He gave me my first radio interview soon after, and he introduced me once again as "a hot new deejay in the making." It was my first interview. He also showcased some of the new records I was spinning at Yesterday.

It was a thrill. The program was also the only Disco show in Boston, which made Luongo the ambassador of Disco in this town. He was also the first Billboard reporter to compile the charts representing that city. He put Boston on the map when it came to the music and eventually moved to New York to became arguably the greatest remixer of all time. He was so great that Epic and the Jacksons, including Michael, used him exclusively for their remixes. But John was more than just a deejay or a remixer. He was an artist. John was just as important in our world as Quincy Jones was as a producer. In our world, he was a superstar. John is easily in the top ten most important people in the history of Disco music and the business. And as supportive as John was of me, he was just as tolerant, which would become very important for me later on.

Chapter 10:

THE CAPE COMES TO BOSTON

One night the Peña brothers showed up nine deep at the door of Yesterday, and everything changed. We had taken a trip to Cape Cod, where we ran into these Cape Verdean guys at a club in Falmouth and became fast friends. Wayne Peña was the one we met first. In no time, he had introduced us to his brothers, cousins, aunts, uncles, voodoo doctors, spiritual consultants, parakeets, and everyone else. The Peñas were everywhere in Falmouth.

Together they ran that town. They looked good, had money, and girls liked them; they were the kind of guys you wanted to be around. In Falmouth, they almost exclusively dated white girls. And I swear, white chicks from Boston went down the Cape just to bang a Peña. Pretty soon we were hanging out with them whenever we had the chance. But it always used to kill me that they insisted they weren't black. "No, we're Cape Verdean," one brother would invariably say.

"Ok, you can be whatever you want to be."

We had been friends for a while, and I thought it was time for them to come to my club. They were my friends, and I wanted them here. I invited Wayne, but family of friends are friends, so they all showed up together one night. They rolled up on Frankie D., who was working the door. Greg was recovering from a stab wound that night, and so Frankie had taken over. This was Frankie's first nightclub job, but he'd eventually evolve from doorman to brilliant restauranteur. He knew they were coming because I had let him know in advance, and he greeted them warmly and welcomed them.

I also knew that what I was doing might not be received well by management, but I didn't care. I was sick of this segregated bullshit in a club that played almost all black music. Of course we didn't play any n****r music, as management called it, but I still didn't understand what that distinction was. I just knew what bothered certain people, and I was always pushing that limit. Now we would see where the limit really was.

I introduced them when they walked in: "Ladies and gentlemen—in particular, ladies—the Peña brothers are here. And I'm sure you can't miss them."

A bunch of people turned around and said "Hey," but then everybody got a good look at them and got stunned for a second. They probably had never seen that many black—err, Cape Verdean—people in a club before.

A few guys already knew the Peña's, so when they went up and said hello, all awkwardness disappeared. The whole group piled up at the bar, and Wayne pulled out a knot of cash as thick as a calzone and started spending money—and more importantly, tipping. They bought rounds of drinks and champagne, and I watched as the white chicks started circling around them. No doubt they loved the money those guys were spending, but I was willing to bet they were all hoping for some big bamboo.

I was also thinking how great it was that all my people were down on the floor having a good time when Frank Melgar walked into the room. He could tolerate a couple black guys, but not nine. He left as quick as he had come and reappeared with a half-dozen bouncers from Lucifer. I saw them march in the back with Frank leading the way, and I jumped out of the booth and cut them off before they reached the floor.

"They're with me, Frank!"

"You should fucking know better, Joe. Get them the fuck outa here!"

"They're my friends!"

"Either they go, or you go!"

"Then I go."

Frank stood there with the meatheads behind him. I turned and jumped back into the booth, clicked on the microphone, and stopped the record, which killed the floor and made everyone look up at me. Frank stood livid off to the side.

"Yo! They don't want my friends in the club, and you all know why. Fuck this shit. If they're out of here, so am I."

I grabbed my records and jumped down from the booth. I almost took a beating myself. Melgar was pissed, and the gorillas with him were ready to get their hands on me. But I walked past them at the bar as I crossed the dance floor, and they stayed put. Nobody was confused about what was going on there. The audience parted as I walked out with the Peña brothers. Then eighty percent of that club followed me.

Frank was going to come to understand that I *was* that club, and those people were there because *I* brought them in. I made an effort every night to establish connections with everybody that walked in the door. Nobody was invisible there, and a lot of regulars came because of that vibe—a vibe that did not exist before me. That's not coming from a place of pride, either. Yesterday was different from other clubs: it was personal, we were a family, and everybody was comfortable. That kind of success takes a group effort. Even when strangers walked in, I did my very best to make them feel like they were on the inside, and they knew it. They felt it. Pretty soon everybody was on the inside. This was their club, so when I walked, they walked with me.

It didn't take very long for management to figure out that they had no real money coming in without me, and so the bartenders and waitresses were pissed. We even gave management a little push by boycotting the club. We were all family, so it was easy to track seventy-five percent of the patrons down. And Frankie D. at the door would tell others who showed up: "He's not here, so don't come in." Then Shelly put together a petition that even the bartenders and waitresses signed, which I appreciated. They didn't have to do that; they could have lost their jobs. Shelly brought the petition back to one of the bartenders who gave it to Frank, and he brought it up to Henry. Even though Frank threw me out, he personally had no problem with black guys in the club; he was doing his job. And that's when they brought me back. Frank called me and asked me to come. When I got to the club, Henry came over to see me, which was a big deal because he almost never came into Yesterday.

"Nice to have you back," he said. Then he told me he was going to open a new club downstairs. "We're going to close Katy's, change the name, renovate it, and open the best Discotheque in Boston. It'll be yours. You'll love it: it's a big club, and we'll install the best sound and light system in the city."

He then bumped my take to $75 a night. There were very few, if any, who made that much in a night as a deejay in Boston.

After that, I was given carte blanche, and I set out to hire a backup deejay—and come hell or high water, he was going to be black.

I held a daytime interview/audition similar to the one I had walked into a few years back, except this one was going to be fixed. I let my buddy Cosmo Wyatt know about the audition on the low. Cosmo spun records at Emerson house parties, and he was a wizard with his portable mobile system, which included a mixer and a turntable. Of course, I was hoping for a fight from management, but nobody said shit. Cosmo was now my new backup deejay for when I needed to step out of the booth to entertain the ladies or needed a night off.

I had won. I was the best deejay in Boston, and I could do whatever I wanted. And all I wanted was to have the best people and dancers partying and spending their dough under one roof, at the best club in Boston. And it was all mine. That was the moment Boston clubs became integrated. Yesterday was the first one, and for a long time the only one, that actually was. And once Katy's closed for good and Celebration opened, we blew the doors off that bullshit forever.

It was also the day I started playing the records I wanted, which included funk. I can't say I was the funkiest deejay in Boston—that honor goes to John Luongo, but I got pretty funky after that. That's not all I played; I tackled all musical genres, but expanding my playlist by 30% enabled me to finally get to the next level as a deejay.

Chapter 11:

EXPERIMENTATION

Yesterday was back in full swing, and Celebration was out in the future. I was in Disco heaven. Everything I ever wanted, blacks and whites and everyone together, funk and other innovative music, was all right there in front of me every night. So what do you do when you think everything's perfect? Explore and expand.

The foundation of Disco was built on gay and black nightclub culture, so I started hitting the gay scene to find out what all the crazy cutting-edge clubs were up to, and finding out what they were playing was important research for keeping us fresh.

I hit the jackpot when I walked into a club John Luongo told me about. It showed me a whole new world. It was called Chaps, located in Boston's South End, a high traffic area tucked behind the Boston Public Library. I had already heard about the deejay who played there, but he was light years better than I thought he would be.

Danae Jacovidis was a pioneer. Born in Pennsylvania, he spent most of his career in Boston. He collaborated with the best of them, John Luongo included, and was both the producer and remixer on several songs and albums that became smashes. "Born to Be Alive" by Patrick Hernandez was one huge hit and is still played today.

When I walked through the door, Danae was playing a song I had never heard before: "Happiness Is Just Around the Bend" by the Main Ingredient. Cuba Gooding Junior's father was the lead singer. It went on to become one of my favorite songs. It seems like a favorite song of mine was playing whenever I walked through a new door, but it just goes to show the way Disco was back then. It was hard to find and hear all the music, especially early on, and different deejays were pioneering records that no one (especially not on radio) had heard before and bringing it to their audience. As always, this meant that in order to find new music, you had to go in search of it.

Out on the floor, I saw guys shirtless and sweating. That floor also represented the stereotypical Bostonian gay guy: clean cut and handsome in jeans, which typified that kind of collegiate homosexual who wasn't as "ostentageous" as those in some of the other scenes, as a grease ball might say. But Chaps was all about the music and the moment, and it wasn't as flamboyant as some of the other clubs like The Otherside, known as OS, a place that made every other gay club around appear tame. An example is that at Chaps, I didn't have to worry about walking across the floor and somebody patting me down, though to be honest, I was kind of disappointed that none of the boys thought I was hot enough to give me a nice ass grab. Of all the gay clubs in Boston, I was most comfortable at Chaps, but I would branch out.

By this point, I was getting used to walking into a club for the sole purpose of feeling out a deejay and his musical prowess, and so without hesitation I walked right up and introduced myself to Danae. I soon found out that there were in fact two Danaes. I got the nasty drunken prick that night. I didn't hold it against him, though. He was too good, and I was having too much fun to let his insolence bother me—so much fun in fact that while out on the floor I yanked off my shirt. I loved it. The passion of the room pulled me in, and I moved along with everybody else. As time went on and I visited Chaps more often, Danae was smiling and friendly almost all of the time when he saw me. But when he was drunk, he was still a bitch.

Danae a.k.a. "Duchess" passed away February 24, 2012. He was sixty-three years old. He left an amazing legacy in Boston, and he was the longest running relevant reporting deejay ever in this town—a career of almost forty years.

A few nights later, I hit up another of the better gay clubs in town. Located at 1270 Boylston St., it was aptly named 1270. I was there to check out the greatest deejay of all time, Jimmy Stuard. Jimmy was from Oklahoma, and he came to Boston to attend MIT. Lucky for us, the Disco gods decided he belonged behind a turntable. He created flawless blends from one record to the next. What distinguished him from everybody else was that he did it from sixteen to twenty beats, and he'd run the blend together for a minute. It was just unheard of. It's one thing to say but another to hear, and Jimmy sounded unbelievable. He obviously had regular blends because his audience knew what was coming, and when they heard the mélange, they went absolutely insane. I myself had no idea what was coming that first night.

At straight clubs you'd always have peaks and valleys; people would walk off the dance floor at those times, and you'd have to work to get them back, no matter how good you were. But in the gay clubs, the energy never seemed to cease, and especially with Jimmy there was never any lull.

I hung out, taking it all in. It was at 1270 that I heard "That Old Black Magic" by the Softones for the first time. Jimmy also treated me to my first double echo, where he played the same record on both turntables with one four beats or so behind the other. I also got passed some amyl nitrate, an inhalant that relaxes your blood vessels and every damn muscle in your body. I had never seen it before, or needed it, because nobody's putting anything in my ass. I tried it anyway—what the hell, "When in Rome," as they say. I floated around like David Blaine after that.

The inhalants and the atmosphere helped me get up the courage to float over and visit Jimmy in his booth. Since my first meeting with Danae, I was worried that Jimmy might be just as rough. But Jimmy was easy and welcomed me into the booth. He gave me a big smile, and he already knew my name from Luongo. My reputation was beginning to precede me, and it was flattering to be known by a legend.

Eventually, West End Records President and Boston guy Mel Cheren saw so much talent in Jimmy that he brought him from Boston and made him the resident deejay of the number one gay club in New York City, 12 West—a club that Mel co-owned. The rivalry musically between the two cities was vicious then, right up there with the Red Sox-Yankees. Now our Boston guy was the number one deejay in New York, and we felt some pride in that fact.

On May 25, 1977, Jimmy Stuard perished in a fire at the Everard Baths on West 28th Street in New York. He is now the resident deejay in heaven's Disco. Saint Peter is his light man.

One of the most shocking things I've ever encountered in a club was in a small corner of the 1270. It was almost like a cubbyhole, with a bunch of guys in collared shirts and Dockers just milling around and looking painfully out of place. There were a lot of younger boys around them who seemed to dress the part and were very comfortable in their surroundings and with themselves. I thought to myself, "What a fucking weird little crew over there." And I asked somebody what was going on.

"That's Cathedral Corner," they said. "That's where all the priests hang out." And they weren't taking confessions either.

I made the 1270 a regular spot on Sunday nights. I loved it there, and it became one of my favorite clubs. And once the guys figured out I wasn't gay, they would hook me up with their girls. Some of the hottest chicks I've ever picked up in my life were scooped up in gay clubs.

There was also something else I noticed. It might've been a gay bar, but there was a very strong showing of straights, Whites, Blacks, Hispanics, even priests, all under one roof and all there for the same reason and sharing the love. They were there for the music and the people that drove it. That's Disco! And that's what I wanted to bring to Yesterday. Except for the priests. I was more of a nun guy myself.

Chapter 12:

POLITICS

My eyes were starting to open, and I was getting wise to the business side of the Boston Disco scene. John Luongo was already talking to various record companies and radio stations, pitching the importance of the deejays and the clubs. We both knew that if someone from a radio station came and saw one of these clubs, they'd realize the overlap with the pop audience, and we could get airplay on radio. That's when my wheels started spinning, and I began thinking about how we could get to be bigger and stronger than we were.

But somebody else beat me to it.

One night an older guy—and by older, I mean in his thirties—walked into Yesterday. He looked cool too. He dressed well and had a tan, but the thing that stuck out most of all was that he was holding records in his hand. I thought he was the new deejay for Lucifer. But that seemed odd, since I hired the new deejays, and I had never seen him.

He put the mystery to bed when he walked up to the booth and introduced himself. "My name's Don Delacey from RCA Records," he said. He reeked like a cannabis nursery.

"Really, wow. What are you doing here?" I had no idea how the business worked at that time, and I had only gotten the slightest glimpse of what this music really could become if the right people got behind it.

Don continued: "I'm the regional rep for RCA. I go to radio every week and ask them to play our new songs. How do you think Vicki Sue Robinson got played on radio?" Vicki Sue Robinson had been a huge hit in the clubs before she got to radio.

"How?" I asked.

"It happened because the clubs in Boston somehow discovered her and were playing her. She was packing the dance floors, and after I saw how big she was, it was easier for me to get her played on the radio. Discos are the next big thing. The labels don't even know it yet. These clubs are going to break a lot of records and a lot of artists before radio even gets to them."

This guy was talkin' my language, and he was in the perfect position to do what I had only just begun to dream of.

He added, "I've got some new records I think will work for you," and then he handed me a bunch of 45s along with a little bag of joints—the source of the smell. Come to find out, record reps had the best of everything, starting with their clothes, their cars, their hookers, and right at the top of the pyramid: drugs. I took those records from Don along with his parting gift and played each one of them back-to-back-to-back.

I was beginning to see the politics of the record business, which had never really affected me before. I was just a guy spinning records I liked. I wasn't really thinking about much else. A rep like Don was like a lobbyist. Instead of running around the Senate, he showed up at clubs, guiding and cajoling and giving out free weed. He'd do whatever he could to get a record played. In order to survive in his business, he needed the instinct for what was hot and what was not, or else nobody would've listened to him. He could see the potential in the Discotheques to make artists blow up, and he hit the ground running to get the records in the doors.

Don stood off to the side beaming as I spun his records. Then he asked me what other clubs he should hit. I gave him a short list. Boston became a massive RCA Records town because they were the first to pay attention to the Boston Discotheque scene. RCA was our number one major label. And from then on, Don, nicknamed Spacey DeLacey, was part of my life.

I thought Don's appearance was going to be an isolated incident as far as record reps went. As it turned out, he was just ahead of the curve, and the other promoters started coming out of the woodwork soon after. From then on, I no longer bought my own records, or coke, or grass, or drinks, or anything else for that matter.

We were moving the dial, and the labels were starting to notice, but I never would've guessed where we were headed next.

Chapter 13:

SEEDBED

She showed up at Yesterday one night, smooth-skinned, cool, and beyond beautiful. She could've been anything: black, white, orange, or paisley, it didn't matter. She was gorgeous, and I wanted her. I saw her the second she walked in. My head was down looking at a record, but something made me look up, and my eyes landed on her.

I sent her a drink. Who wouldn't? If some asshole from across the bar buys a woman a drink, chances are she'd drain the whole thing without ever making eye contact with him. If the deejay sends one, that's a little different. I knew this, and it worked. Pulling these girls was included in my salary, and the waitresses were like my wingmen. I had no problem asking them to bring drinks to different women. I think it brought them back to high school, but instead of passing notes, they passed cocktails. They would either deliver drinks or sidle up to the girl and say, "Hey, Joe wants to buy you a drink."

"Who's Joe?"

"He's the deejay."

The girls would look up at me then. I'd wink. Dead serious, if they told me I couldn't do it anymore, I would've quit and found another venue more conducive to my program.

I watched the handoff between this knockout and the waitress from my post. She handed her the drink and jerked her thumb over her shoulder in my direction. The woman then stood up and glided toward me, cool as all hell. Her dark eyes, which assessed me like a target, told me she was going to be a problem. Fine with me.

"Thanks for the drink, my name's Nanci." She was even better looking up close, which in this room was not always the case. After introducing herself, she asked a question that for me was the straw that broke the camel's back.

"Can you play 'Swearin' to God'?"

"Frankie Valli?" I loved her for asking me to play that record. It made her even that much more extraordinary. I was crazy about her.

That night was the beginning of a personal relationship that's lasted over 40 years. She was the first black chick I had ever been with, and she was a tough act to follow. But as to the music, that Frankie Valli record she requested went on to become the most requested record of 1975, which is impressive considering it didn't come out until May. That song was important for another reason as it marked a major change in the music itself. It was the point when the mainstream started making the transition to Disco. We were right on the cusp of a revolution, and "Swearin' to God" was like Paul Revere: "Disco is coming! Disco is coming!"

It also happened to be the first song that I can distinctly point to and say that I was the first deejay to report the record in my top ten to *Record World*, a music industry trade publication. I didn't break the record all by myself, but I did play it first, and when I did, I knew it was going to be huge. I even took the time to introduce it on the dance floor, something I rarely did.

"The first person on the dance floor that can tell me who does this gets free drinks," I said. Would you believe it, within ten seconds some meatball turned around and yelled, "What the fuck, kid, it's Frankie Valli."

"That's it. Give my *coosheen* here three free drinks."

All the grease balls turned around then. There was nothing bigger at that time than Frankie Valli in a room full of Italian Americans. The song went over right away. But a lot of deejays didn't want to touch it because it was from Frankie, and as a general rule white artists didn't get played in the club at that time. But it was a defining moment for us because "Swearin' to God" was both by a white artist and hit the clubs before it hit Top 40 Radio. Frankie Valli and the Four Seasons hadn't had a hit since Valli's 1967's solo smash, "Can't Take My Eyes Off You." This is a perfect example of how a '60s act had a new avenue to bring them back. This also applies to a laundry list of R&B acts.

It used to be that you went out and caught a live band, which was an event in itself. But when the clubs started breaking records, going out to Yesterday and hearing a song you'd never heard before and knowing that you couldn't hear it anywhere else because nobody else had it was a whole new type of event. Everyone knows the thrill of discovering new music, especially music heads. But with the labels now feeding us records, we had all the music before it came out anywhere. So if you wanted to be at the cutting edge and you liked to party and dance, then you went to one of a few Discotheques in town that were in the loop.

The Discotheque was now a new kind of creature when it came to promoting acts and breaking music, and guys like Don Delacey were making sure of that. We also didn't really call the Discotheques "Discos" yet either; they were Discotheques or clubs. Maybe if you needed space on your advertisement, you'd shorten the word to "Disco," but I still have some of those flyers from '74, '75, '76, and they all read, "Discotheque." Sometimes we'd use the term "Disco Music," but that referred to the music you heard at the Discotheque, not a specific genre.

When the change happened specifically is impossible to know, although the Trammps *Disco Inferno* played a major role, it was largely a slow evolution, and suddenly hardly anyone knew what a Discotheque was anymore. Newcomers only knew of it as a Disco. And the music that promoters and labels started gearing toward the clubs, they called "Disco Music."

At the same time that black acts were getting mainstream recognition, white pop acts like Frankie Valli began putting out "Disco" tracks and crossing over in the other direction, creating huge radio hits that were made for the clubs. But it took years for all of this to work itself out.

We were now the new seedbed. We crossed acts over to Top 40 pop radio like the Trammps, the Savannah Band, the Three Degrees, and KC and the Sunshine Band. We were also responsible for breaking one of the top five female artists of all time and the number one selling, most played artist of the mid-late '70s, Donna Summer. She was so big that she made the cover of Newsweek magazine in 1979. She was *the* face of Disco. In the entire history of *Soul Train*, Don Cornelius only had one co-host, and that was Donna Summer. And every one of those hits came to radio from the clubs. Now the labels no longer needed to lean exclusively on radio to break these acts.

The record labels had a new venue dropped in their laps. And the reps who had a good hustle and "got it" jumped on it. The record company reps who didn't get it could never catch up with the guys who did because we always remembered that they ignored us in the beginning. When we got big, it was payback time for those radio reps who laughed at us like we were a joke. But some of the casualties of this war would bitterly come back to haunt us when they banded together with the Rock 'n' Rollers to kill off Disco, though they did it in name only.

Of course we were breaking and crossing-over new acts in the Discotheques, and this added an entirely new facet for the labels to understand and to exploit. The exception to the rule was Motown because Berry Gordy already positioned his acts as way more than just black acts. From the beginning, they were groomed and positioned as pop artists. And they had huge white audiences. The music they made was unmistakably R&B, but they were pop artists at their core. The biggest records to come out of Motown were all pop records. Acts like the Temptations, the Supremes, and the Four Tops were multi-format right out of the box.

With that said, Motown still used the clubs. Berry Gordy saw the importance of the Discotheques and used them when it was appropriate. A perfect example of his objective was when the clubs broke Thelma Houston's remake of Harold Melvin and the Blue Notes, "Don't Leave Me This Way."

At this point, John Luongo proved that he was smarter than everyone because when the local reps wouldn't work with us, or were hesitant to, Luongo went over their heads to the labels and explained to them why the local reps were dropping the ball. They took what he said into consideration, but rather than making their local guys look bad, the record labels took it upon themselves to talk directly with John Luongo, which was huge. Not only did that strengthen us, but that also positioned John to launch his monumental remix/reproduction career.

Once he established a connection with the labels, he started the Boston Record Pool. Boston had the first record pool in the country to charge a fee by supplying records to deejays throughout New England. It became a "one-stop shop" for the record companies, so they no longer had to service all of the deejays individually but could just service the record pool instead.

John's pitch was simple. He told the labels: "Super serve all the deejays in Boston. Radio is tuning into the clubs, and you never know which club a radio deejay might walk into." He explained that there were another twenty-five or thirty deejays popping up outside of Boston in the suburbs, and they needed to be serviced too. "For convenience's sake, I'll open an office, and you'll service me. The deejays will become members in our record pool, and once a week they'll come in to pick up records and fill out a feedback sheet for last week's record. This way we can track them."

The record labels agreed, and John charged thirty dollars a month to each of the deejays for organizing it. Thirty dollars was a good deal for the deejays too because it saved them the expense of going out and buying all the records themselves, when we were spending a minimum of sixty dollars a month on records to keep on top of things. John also made me director of the record pool.

Here's where it gets sticky. When money is changing hands, and you have a kid from East Cambridge in the mix—that kid being me—you better believe at that age that I would sniff out a scam and find a way to take advantage. And that's exactly what I did.

There was a used record store downstairs from the record pool called Nuggets—a lucky coincidence. When I saw that, a light bulb went off. I then met with John and told him that we should order extra promos, which were free records from the labels, so we could have them around as a library or if some of the members wanted a second copy to play back and forth. He agreed, and so did the labels, and I bumped up our promo order from thirty-five to fifty of each record, ten of which I inherited on the down low.

At the end of the day, I went downstairs and sold the extra promos at Nuggets. I was getting two dollars for extended singles (now called twelve-inchers) and five for albums. I looked at it as a light skimming off the top without biting into profits. It wasn't stealing; it was individual creative Disco financing. That was my story, and I stuck with it, but I was starting to spin my tires. Drugs didn't run my life then, now, or ever, but they were becoming such a part of my everyday routine that getting fucked up was limiting me in ways I didn't like, and with all the money, craziness, and free drugs, I was making bad decisions.

CHAPTER 14:

LUCIFER'S INFERNO

As the Disco movement surged forward, it was simultaneously showing its age; it would eventually suffer an overexposure that would make it passé—many thanks Travolta and *Saturday Night Fever*. But the burnout was over the horizon, and for the moment we were basking in the bright lights—literally.

One night I was working the booth, dropping the needle on record after record, but my mind was elsewhere. The number one Disco act in the world was playing next door at Lucifer and I was stuck working the booth at Yesterday. I already knew I'd see them later backstage, and I had plans on seeing their second show the following night, but for now I was bogged down with responsibility.

My night suddenly turned around when the Kenmore club's co-manager, John Beale, came bursting through the connector door with a look of alarm on his face that told me there was trouble.

"Joe, Joe, Joe. You gotta come over. You gotta come here, now!" He shouted when he got to my booth.

My co-resident deejay, Calvin "Cosmo" Wyatt, was in the club, and so I motioned for him to come up. Cosmo was always a choirboy: never chased skirts, never did drugs, and I never saw him have a drink. He is now an ordained minister.

"Can you handle this?" I said.

"No problem," he scoffed.

I followed John through the connector door to Lucifer with no idea what to expect when I got there. Anything could happen. It was a mob bar after all. Plenty of times one guy would owe another guy money and some poor *strunz* would get slapped around on the dance floor. Degenerate gamblers used to tip the doorman and say, "Listen, if Tookie the bookie comes here tonight, give me a heads up. I'll be by the back." Or Brian Wallace, Henry Vara's partner, might go crazy on somebody. He was mostly an asshole. And he was always skating on his ankles. He looked like a shit-faced, white-haired leprechaun, but built like a brick shit house. Brian was the kind of guy who could have eight drinks and be 100%, but that ninth drink would send him over the edge. All you had to do was catch his eye the wrong way, and he'd be all over you. And if you looked at his girlfriend, you'd catch a beating. And she was a gorgeous, light-skinned black girl, with a balcony out to here, so beatings were passed out on the regular.

Lucifer was about as close to 100% wise guy as you could get, real Italian, with the exception of Freddy Jones the Player, and TY the pimp, and some fellas from the Winter Hill Gang, including the Irish Kingpin, Howie Winters, and the infamous Whitey Bulger.

But I wasn't concerned with their clientele tonight. I walked past two of the gorillas they had at the door and saw why I had been summoned. My friend Ruffy Mugica was dangling by his leg from the ten-foot steel ladder that led up to the deejay booth. The booth was set up like a theater box, but you didn't enter it from the back; instead you had to climb up a ladder to get in. I got Ruffy the job working that deejay booth, but he'd get so fucked up he couldn't even get down. On more than one occasion, they left Ruffy up there with a bucket and locked the club up rather than bothering to pull him out. But not tonight. Don't get me wrong—Ruffy wasn't a drunk; he just couldn't hold his liquor. He was a bad deejay sober and even worse when he was shit-faced.

It was obvious what had happened. For whatever reason, Ruffy had decided he needed to climb down, but he fell and got his leg caught between the rungs. Obviously, the guys left him there because it looked hilarious, and instead of helping out they were helping themselves to his change off the floor and, of course, mocking him relentlessly. "Hey, yo Ruffy, you oughta try playin' records upside down, maybe you'd sound better!"

I took pity on him, briefly. "You fucking guys," I said. "What the fuck. Give me a hand." I climbed a few feet up the ladder with one of the gorillas and we lifted Ruffy up and pulled him off the ladder. Then we sat him down in a chair. "Get him some fuckin' coffee or the other thing, would ya? Get this stumbling prick back on his feet." I turned to Ruffy and said, "Ruffy, you drunk fuck, you ok?"

He stood up and said: "Who you callin' a drunk?"

I put my finger on his forehead and lightly pushed, and he fell back into the chair.

Ruffy and I were close friends. He came out with the crew every night and was a legendary dancer in the clubs. He eventually went to Vegas, where he was the in-house entertainment at the Riviera.

When I saw he was fine, I turned and climbed the ladder and put on the next record. Tonight the deejay was just the warm-up for the Trammps who were coming soon anyway, and since Ruffy took that spill, I was forced to stay in place and watch them perform. Now I'd get to see them two nights in a row.

They were the biggest Disco act in the world then and were riding two massive records, "That's Where the Happy People Go" and "Disco Inferno," which crossed them over to pop radio. But they weren't new to the game. They already had big R&B records, most of which were classic, first-generation Disco hits like "Zing Went the Strings of My Heart," and "Where Do We Go From Here."

I wasn't exactly dressed to be in Lucifer though. I had on an orange mohair sweater over a collared shirt and jeans with pleats so sharp you could cut tomatoes. And I had enough Niagara spray starch on them that the fabric didn't bend, it broke. I was ironed and starched for Lucifer, but that's about it, because this was a suit and tie place. But under the circumstances, they let my casual clothing slide.

I spun a few more records and took every request; when you got a request at Lucifer, you played it. Naturally, some grease ball wanted to hear "Fly Robin Fly," and so I played that several times.

When the time came, I introduced the Trammps. "Ladies and Gentlemen, direct from Philadelphia, the world's number one Disco act, the Trammps." The band jumped on stage dressed in purple semi-tuxedos with ruffled shirts and bow ties. The drummer, Earl Young, who was the leader of the act, settled in behind his kit, and their emcee, Flash, pumped up the crowd. The band played the Trammps Disco theme, which was an instrumental, and I watched the brass and horns reflect the stage lights. The crowd got into a frenzy. Then Ruffy climbed the ladder and stood beside me.

"I can take over," he said. "I'm good now, I'm good." He'd had his coffee and had taken a walk, and he felt sober enough not to fall out of the booth and onto the dance floor. His new semi-sobriety meant I could get out of there, and since Cosmo was deejaying next door, then I could go down on the floor and get crazy with the Trammps. This was turning out to be a nice night for me.

I jumped out of that booth as fast as I could. Everybody was going nuts, except for the hard-core, old-school spaghetti heads who stayed seated in the back with their whores. Every once in a while, you'd hear them shout: "Hey, sit the fuck down," to somebody in front of them who blocked their view.

Pushing through the throng, I spotted my friend Lisa. She was one of our crew. It was unusual for crews to have girls in them. Some would have girls they passed around, but that wasn't the case for Lisa, or Shelly—they were one of us. We were mixed, even from different neighborhoods and cultures.

We had Paul Morales the Puerto Rican; and Ricky Maciejko, he was half Polack from East Cambridge; and Wayne Peña, a.k.a. Billy Dee, at least he thought so; and Manny Marcanos, the Venezuelan who you couldn't understand a word from; and Georgie Borden and Johnny Coppola; and Errol Hall who claimed to be from England but was actually from Jamaica; and Nicky the Gypsy. Of course, add to that list the menace and fuck-a-holic, Lupo, and the two Jew broads Lisa and Shelly rounded it out. It was amazing we all got along because out of that list there were four drug dealers. Lisa was the go-between and kept things smooth, so everyone played nice. And in the club, she was the one-stop for the *hookie dookie* and whatever else you needed. She was a standup chick too—she never skated you and she never skimmed off the top.

Lisa and I saw each other at the same time. We both had the same thing in mind and weaseled our way to the front, right along the stage, to watch the Trammps. After a few songs, they came with their premier song at that time, "Disco Inferno"—the track that settled what the music and clubs would be known as forever. Everybody knew the song, so people were wild. But when the song came to the crescendo, "Burn baby burn," and they popped the pyrotechnics, I went up like a Roman Candle.

Can lights ran the outside of the stage, but unbeknownst to me the can right in front of me was a flash pod. The stage crew had pulled the flash pods off the back of the stage where they would typically be because management was afraid the walls would catch fire when they popped. That's because even the walls were carpeted. This was the seventies after all, and anything that could get carpeted got carpeted. I'm surprised they didn't carpet the ladder rungs—maybe people wouldn't have fallen off so much.

When the can in front of me popped, it knocked me on my ass. All I saw was a white and orange flash, and then I smelled burnt hair. I had no idea what happened. I thought it happened to somebody else. But I was on the floor, and Lisa was screaming, "Holy shit, he's on fire!" Then people lifted me up.

"You alright, you alright?" I didn't know what to say. I didn't know if I was all right. I had to take a look.

All the while, the fucking Trammps didn't miss a beat. They kept right on playing while all this happened right in front of them. The guys that grabbed me started walking me to the door leading to Yesterday.

"He's alright. Just get him out of here. Get him out of here!" somebody shouted. The staff wanted to rush me out because they didn't want the crowd to panic. Not that they cared for me. I know Henry Vara let out a sigh of relief when he saw it was one of his employees that got hit rather than one of his patrons—the fuck that he was.

The guys quickly hustled me back toward Yesterday. Shelly saw me at that point and immediately screamed in horror. The rest of the crowd in the hallway weren't so charitable, as I could tell by the sound of laughter. It was then that I noticed my hands had taken some burns. After seeing that, I didn't know how bad I was going to be. When they got me to a mirror, I couldn't believe what I saw. My orange mohair was charred black. My mustache, eyebrows, and the front of my beautiful long hair were all white and burnt. But even with all the soot that covered my skin and that unmistakable smell of burnt hair that followed me for several days, I was surprisingly unscathed. I splashed water on my face, took off my sweater, gave up on my hair, and got back to work. A few minutes later, I jumped into the booth to relieve Cosmo. After he looked me up and down with a smirk, he got out of the booth, and I wrapped up the night with some second degree burns on my hands and face. It gave me a nice dash of color, like I went into a tanning bed and stayed a little bit too long.

At the end of the night, I went to get my envelope. When I went up there, I knew the Trammps were getting theirs too. Earl Young sat in the inner office with Henry Vara. The rest of the members of the Trammps, including lead singer Jimmy Ellis, milled around in the outer office with the door between them open.

When I walked in, Ellis looked up at me. Then he pointed and sang, "Burn baby burn!" and everybody in the two rooms started hysterically laughing. I got a kick out of it too, but I never played that song again.

Chapter 15:

CELEBRATION

We were no longer the back-alley club with the tiny dance floor and the secret portal to the backdoor of Lucifer. Yesterday was just that: Yesterday. Just like Henry had said he would, he shut down KKK Katy's and turned the space into the greatest club in Boston. And we ran Celebration like a top.

Henry promoted the head bouncer to run the place, Paul Zach. Paul and I were tight. He was a really nice guy, but if you crossed him the Hulk would come out, and you did not want to get knuckled by this guy. He kicked more ass than I could ever care to count. Back then, people could beat the shit out of each other without getting sued or arrested, but every once in a while, somebody would call the cops.

"I just got beat up in Celebration."

The cops would show up, but we were always ready. We'd run up to the safe room above Lucifer and sit tight. The cops knew about the safe room, but they weren't talking. They'd just let the guy blow off some steam.

They'd bring the accuser into Celebration and let him look around a bit. "Well? Do you see him?"

"No."

"Then there's nothin' we can do for you."

And that was it. No problem. We'd come down from the safe room and go about our business. Later that night, you'd find the same boys in blue in Henry's office waiting for an envelope, not one bit shy about what they were doing either.

In the meantime, what we feared most was coming to be. Disco was crossing over and going mainstream. Between Donna Summer, the Trammps, and the Village People, Disco became a household word. The writing was on the wall when I stopped by my mom's and she had Barry White and Donna blaring through her kitchen cassette player. Every Italian kitchen had something cooking on the stove and a cassette player right next to it. I never thought I'd live to hear "Hot Stuff" being belted out in my mom's house. Everything I got hassled for my entire youth—the music, the lifestyle, the affection for black and gay artists—was suddenly picked up by everybody who had busted my balls just for liking different shit. The mainstream was here.

And much to my disgust, the view from my booth was no longer of a foxy room of well-dressed women in wrap dresses or tight and perfectly fitted bellbottoms but of a sea of ill-fitting spandex, untailored corduroy jumpsuits, and...cellulite. We were standing on the edge of commercialization. I was practically grief-stricken. The first-generation club-goers weren't outnumbered by the upstarts and wannabes yet—everything still had that small, intimate family feel to it—but we were being infiltrated, there was no mistaking it; like when some out-of-towner buys your best friend's house and turns it into a condo, you can see the writing on the wall.

Long gone were the days of Zelda and the suit and tie Disco. The new generation of Disco was redefining the style and the music. Disco now appealed to the masses—the thirty-five and over demographic was getting into it, and that can dull the shine on anything.

Once they saw *Saturday Night Fever*, it was all over for us, but more on that later.

The Discotheque (which was now just the Disco), the look, the style, the sound, became ubiquitous. Everywhere you looked, people of all ages were stealing the style in small ways, cheapening the value of the whole era. Radio caught up as well. Radio and Discotheque deejays now got serviced at the same time, making it more and more difficult to break new music and artists in the clubs since radio had the music at the same moment. We weren't special anymore. We were responsible for disco's existence, and now we had to wait in line like everyone else. It was a total kick in the balls. Then some newbie would request a song that broke on the radio, and it was all I could do not to boomerang the record into their neck: "Go home and listen to it on the radio—get the fuck away from my booth!"

At this time, the Village People were *the* ultimate mainstream group. Most of the members were gay, and they had a massive audience. It was like Liberace times ten. From gay teenage boys to bored housewives, they were booming out of every radio in the country. Even the average five-year-old was obsessed with "YMCA."

Even though they had a mainstream vibe, and had that mainstream, radio audience, we had a lot of love for the group.

And then one night, out of nowhere, they showed up at the club. It was the meeting of worlds—when a mainstream act showed up at a Boston club for fun. And they had only given us a little bit of notice too, just to build our excitement.

Paul Zach could barely contain himself when they arrived. "They're here, they're here!"

"Now?"

"Yeah! A couple of limos just pulled up. You want me to have them come in the back door?"

"Nah, don't do that. Have 'em come through the front, through the crowd. They'll fuckin' love it," I said.

Suddenly there was a ruckus, and the crowd turned in the direction of the noise. Over their heads I saw a colorful bouncing headdress, and then it registered with everybody else. The crowd knew exactly who it was and went bananas. I didn't have to announce them because who else could it be?

I got on the mic and said, "Yo, make a lane, get 'em up here. Come on up here fellas—you too, Felipe."

We cleared the dance floor because we didn't have a stage for them to perform on. Members at the time were: The Cop, Victor Willis, who was the token straight guy and lead vocalist. Sometimes he switched it up and performed as a naval officer. Glenn Martin Hughes, in tight leather, was The Biker. He was a highway toll collector when he was discovered. Randy Jones, The Cowboy, was on vocals. He was the sweetest guy—there's no other way to describe him. I liked him, and we kept in touch. There was also David Hodo, The Construction Guy, and Alex Briley, The GI Guy, the very quiet and talented son of a minister. And then, Felipe Rose, The Indian. And Felipe *was* The Village People and a legitimate Native American, Lakota Sioux. He was also a certifiable maniac.

Felipe was all fucked up when he showed up, and he got on the mic and began hyping the crowd. I told everybody to stand back a little farther off the dance floor so the guys had space to move around. They started right in with "Macho Man," and the place freaked out. The crowd sang word for word the whole way through. After that song, they kept the energy up with "YMCA" and "San Francisco."

This was probably the highest population of gays we ever had in the club at one time. Their absence wasn't due to any prejudice, but the gay crowd felt they really couldn't be themselves in Celebration. They could be in Yesterday to a degree, but this new place was just too big, and they didn't want to spend all their time at a "breeder" club when there were plenty of places that they could just be free and comfortable and take off most of their clothes.

In the middle of one of the songs, Victor invited everybody onto the dance floor and then jumped onto a cocktail table to finish the song while the crowd vibrated around him. In the midst of all this, Lupo danced with the Indian on the floor. He cock teased the Village People. It was like they had another member for a minute, The Obnoxious Italian, Lupo.

Carl usually did whatever he wanted, whenever and wherever he wanted to do it. The Loop didn't give a fuck—never did and never will. His signature move was to spin girls and let them go flying into a table, knocking all the drinks over, sometimes injuriously, while he grabbed another girl and just kept on dancing.

Anytime I heard a crash, I knew it was him.

He was a big hit with the Village People that night, and you could just feel they were having fun with the audience. Here's a bunch of gay guys of various ethnicities winning over a crowd like we had. Everything I wanted in a club was right here, happening in front of me, and I helped build it.

When the Village People were done, they mingled with the crowd. Running around, taking pictures, drinking, screaming, hollering, and dancing. It was a *stellah* night. They were having so much fun they didn't want to leave. But they had to put in an appearance at the 1270.

As they left, I gave them the address to our new place, an apartment right across the street from the Kenmore.

"Listen, we like to party at my place after last call, you should come by."

I never expected they would actually show up.

Later that night, there was a knock on the door, and Shelly answered. In the hallway stood Felipe the Indian and Randy the

Cowboy. A few of our after-hours regulars showed up as well, and we hit it hard all night.

Of course, Lupo ended up with his shirt off, wearing the Cowboy's hat and dancing with Felipe.

"You keep it up, Carl," I said at one point, "and you're gonna end up with a peace pipe in your ass."

When the sun came up, Felipe gave Shelly his anklet with bells on it. Everybody kissed each other goodnight. From start to finish, it was off the hook.

Off the record, every now and again I still put the bells on and bop around the room to "Macho Man."

CHAPTER 16:

MOOSE CROSSING DISCO

Anything you ever imagined happening in New York or LA in the '70s was going on right down the street from Fenway Park. My own back-yard suddenly became a place where the biggest names in Disco would show up and perform at a local club that didn't even have a stage. Unfortunately for me, I was losing my grip. I was too crazy, geeked out, and fucked up to be even remotely aware of what was happening to me. I was like a wild animal.

One Friday afternoon, ahead of a long weekend and in broad daylight, I decided it would be a good idea to break into the record pool by climbing through the front window on the busiest street in Boston. I don't really remember a planning phase for the heist, or even what my escape route would have been or what I intended to steal. The stereo maybe? I definitely wasn't dressed for robbery, and the long hair and fluorescent orange T-shirt that said "I'm a stupid prick" was bound to attract attention.

Of course someone saw me and called the cops.

They showed up like the SWAT team and stormed the building with guns drawn—a rowdy pack of pink-faced Irishmen. I wondered briefly if they liked Disco. They wondered A) what planet I was from, and B) what the fuck I was on.

I didn't know what to say or do, so I dropped the stereo, hit the floor, and lied my ass off, "I work here! I swear to God," I shouted. "I lost my keys and I had to get in."

Did they buy it? I thought maybe they did, but they knew something was wrong.

"Let me call my boss. He'll come down here and straighten this out." My boss was John Luongo.

John did come down and smoothed everything out for me, but when they left, he unloaded. He was pissed. "That's it. I can't do this anymore, Joe. You can't shit where you eat, Joe. You need to stop fucking up. You need to stop doing so many fucking drugs, slow down on the blow," but then in the middle of going off on me, he suddenly stopped as if something had come to mind. "You need a change of scenery," he said in a kinder tone, and then he looked me over some more. I was confused, but then he added, "I'm working on something that will be perfect for you and give you the time to get away."

He had been discussing the possibility of bringing me to New York with him, where he would eventually make his mark remixing and producing records, but that was dead in the water now. While he didn't want to go anywhere with me, he also didn't want to totally get rid of me either. He also loved me like a little brother and was freaked out by my most recent escapade and steady downward spiral.

That's when he offered me a deal that would send me to the North Country for a while. His big idea was to ship me off to Waterville, Maine to build a Disco at a Howard Johnson. Their management had recently pitched John the idea, and now, since he figured I could use some time away, not to mention the money, he offered me an out. It could have been worse, I thought. I also knew he was right and that I needed the time away.

I guess Luongo figured that living amongst lobstermen and lumberjacks in the tall pines of Maine would offer me a kind of rehab; that maybe with less of everything to get in trouble with I would be able to stay out of my own way.

What happened next went quickly. Ted Fields, the entertainment director (or something like that) for Howard Johnson, flew me to Maine in a little Cessna. Flying commercial is a walk in the park compared to going up in one of those little planes. I shit bricks the whole flight, and my anxiety went through the roof as we made our approach to the airport. I should say, instead of an approach, that we suddenly discovered that it was time to land, as the last hour of the flight had been made through heavy cloud cover. I'm not sure how competent Ted was at flying blind as we were since, when he dropped us down out of the clouds, he was surprised that we were right on top of the little airfield outside of Waterville, Maine.

"Oh, Shit!" he said, "There's the airport."

I grabbed the edge of my seat as he banked to get the plane on the right path to the runway. Despite the sudden approach, our landing went fine, though honestly, I could have used something to calm me down after we hit the ground, but we had a schedule to keep after all. After making a couple of jokes, we made our way to his car, and within an hour we had arrived off I-95 at the local HoJos. He acted a little embarrassed when we got there, but I thought it was fine. The location for the club, which they had named Cecil B's, was in the barroom attached to the motel with its own separate entrance, and it was almost ready to open by the time we walked in; a crew had already been working for months turning the bar into a proper Discotheque. Everything was keyed in and ready to go. I hardly had to do a thing. This was even better than I thought, and I told Ted that, which put a smile on his face because I think he was beginning to wonder if I was going to even accept the job. Especially after our little plane ride. But Cecil B's was a perfect setup for me, and incidentally for Carl too, because we didn't have to do a thing but get the people there.

It was a good spot—small, held seventy-five people or so (maybe we could squeeze in a hundred), but they had done it up right. I was impressed. The deejay booth was a few steps off the dance floor across from the bar, and the sound system was perfect for that size club. The lighting was on point too. A key factor driving their decision to open the club was that we were located right off the highway and a few minutes or so away from Colby College, which would give us a steady supply of young patrons. This was also the trouble with the location, since the locals were all related rednecks who wanted nothing to do with Disco and its culture. What that meant was that, while we could pack out the club for the weekends, our main clientele was comprised of bookworms who didn't leave the dorms on weeknights. We could only corrupt them so much and couldn't ever get that weeknight going, and that's where clubs pay the bills.

I didn't think of this at the time. I just took in all the positive features and was happy to get out of Boston with a fresh start. Plus, opening a new club out in the hinterland was fun. I went back home with big plans.

Within a few weeks, I was back up in Waterville with my co-manager/babysitter, Carl Lupo, which in hindsight wasn't the best idea. But just because we were destined to bring madness to the Pine Tree State didn't mean we weren't also going to do our jobs. We put on a professional face, but it wouldn't take a fortune teller to predict that it was only a matter of time before we were in trouble. We didn't know any other way. The only question was, how bad it would be?

In the meantime, I got broken in to life in Maine and its differences from the city pretty quickly. Within a day or so of moving into our three adjoining rooms, I heard a noise outside the window. The clock said 11:00 a.m., and I wondered if Lupo was out behind the motel for some ridiculous reason. But it was early for either of us to be awake. I yawned and pulled back the shades. The light was harsh, and I squinted for a second, but there was no confusing what I was looking at. I was face to face with a bull moose. It was late September then and getting cold in those mountains, so the moose were coming down to eat. There was plenty of green grass and weeds around the motel for them to dine on. All told, and counting antlers, this moose stood over ten-foot tall, and he was giving me the stink eye through the tiny pane of glass. Thank God it wasn't mating season.

After recovering from my close encounter, the first order of business was to start getting the word out. We had a little over a week to do the job. Right off the bat, we spotted an easy way to advertise the operation. Just out front of the motel I spotted a yellow traffic sign that read, "Moose Crossing."

I pointed it out to Lupo.

"They're not kidding," I said.

And that's when we got the idea of writing the word "Disco" in large letters at the bottom of the sign with an arrow pointing in the direction of the club so that everyone who drove by read, "Moose Crossing Disco," with the sign for Cecil B's not far away.

I thought changing the sign was a great idea. In fact, lots of people who showed for the opening night said they loved the "Moose Crossing Disco" sign. The local authorities, however, didn't feel quite the same way about it as we did, and they took it down just after the club opened and then contacted our management with a complaint and a fine. It was obvious who had done that to the sign. That was our first strike, but at the time we didn't think much about it since it was more important for us to get people in the club than it was to worry about a stupid citation.

The collateral damage was that the move turned the local staff against us on day one, and that was a fight that would go on to the very day we were escorted out of town. They didn't want us there anyway, and almost nothing we did could have endeared those people to us. We were city folk. These were country bumpkins, all related, and still using Old Spice. They weren't Disco fans either. But it turned out that the Colby College kids were, and we had great inter-actions with the students as we papered their campus with flyers. We put the flyers everywhere too: cars, telephone poles, and bathroom stalls. We also got them into the hands of as many girls as we could find. For the most part, they seemed starved for a club like this one.

We felt like culture bearers shedding light in the wilderness with a bag of Quaaludes, letting the locals know their nightlife was about to improve. On top of the college, we hit every local bar we could find to pass out flyers and went to nearby towns and put them onto cars and onto any other surface that didn't move.

Besides spreading the word about Cecil B's, we chased girls. The two went hand in hand. But in Waterville, Maine, the pickings were definitely slim, as you might imagine. Even so, we didn't make out so bad. Who could resist two Boston guys with a Howard Johnson's expense account?

After spending the week in town and getting to know the place, we were a little worried about the whole idea, but then opening night Friday came, and we were jammed. The line was down the block.

Carl played doorman and carnival barker, standing out in front of the entrance singing the songs to the girls and bringing a kind of mayhem that was infections for people out looking for a good time. He set the tone, and it worked.

I met a couple new friends that night too. At one point, when I put on a long song, a skinny college kid came up the steps to my booth. I always gave people a chance when they wanted to talk to the DJ and never pulled that attitude on them like I had experienced at Zelda. He introduced himself as Tom Silverman. "It's nice to finally meet you," he said, "I used to go see you down in Boston at Yesterday." He was from New York, but he was going to school up here at Colby. He went on to say that he was graduating this year and that he wanted to start a Disco magazine. "I'll call it Disco News," he said, and he wanted to know if I could help him. I thought it was a good idea and gave him my number. As it turned out, Tom did start that magazine, but then a few years later he went on to found Tommy Boy records, which, by '82, would have legendary hits like Soul Sonic Force's "Planet Rock" and go onto become one of the most successful independent record labels of all time. Who knew he would start everything at Cecil B's in Waterville fucking Maine?

Our antics aside, the club became a hit and put that HoJo's back in the black. This meant management didn't mind what we were doing as long as we kept the money coming in, and we were doing that and then some.

But then Lupo got sick. He hadn't been feeling well. He kept complaining of stomach cramps and was having trouble going to the bathroom. I offered him the usual Italian solution: a bottle of prune juice. "This oughta make you go," I said. But it didn't help. One afternoon, Carl started passing blood, but he refused to go to the doctor. I didn't feel good about the decision, but I didn't force him to go. Then the next afternoon when he didn't wake up, I started banging on his door to get in the room and got no answer. I didn't have the key, so I had to take it from the front desk.

When I finally got inside, I found Lupo lying in bed looking greenish grey. I thought he was dead. I panicked and started shaking him and yelling. He woke up, and that's when I noticed the rancid smell. Looking around, I could see blood on the toilet through the open bathroom door. At that point, he was going to the hospital whether he liked it or not, and I threw him on my shoulder fireman style, took him out the back door to the parking lot, and shoved him inside the passenger side of his car.

At the hospital, we found out he was suffering from diverticulitis. They took him into emergency surgery and removed about nine inches of his colon. It was a happy ending. Then the fun started.

Lupo had a private room, and so I went out and imported a couple of strippers from Portland, about an hour away, to come down and put on a little show for Carl. One of the props they brought was a ten-inch double-headed dildo. Carl was appreciative, but he couldn't get it up because he was on so many drugs. The girls had fun and kissed him goodbye but forgot to take their dildo with them. They left it sitting in the sink.

When I discovered it a couple hours later, Carl laughed. I could tell he had some plan because he was grinning like he had found a bag of joints.

"Give it to me," he said, and he took the Dildo, put it under his gown, and told me to call the doctor, which I did.

"What's the matter?" the doctor asked when he arrived.

"Something happened overnight, doc. I don't know if it's a side effect from the medications or what, but it's got me worried."

"Well, what is it?"

I could barely keep a straight face as Carl pulled open his gown where he had the dildo positioned so one end was dangling between his legs. "Look!" he shouted. "What happened to my prick?" The doctor almost shit himself. Lupo broke out laughing. That was a beautiful sound to hear after thinking he had died in the night.

Carl healed up pretty quickly, and we went back to running the club. We were having a dynamite time under the circumstances, but we weren't winning any popularity contests. We were the wise guys here, surrounded by hunters, trappers, woodchippers and the like.

The coolest guy there was cool because he wore a Members Only jacket.

On New Year's Eve, we had set a couple hundred pounds of confetti in the ceiling to drop when the clock struck midnight. When midnight came, however, we pulled the string to unleash the confetti, and it came down in large clumps of paper—knocking people down, spilling drinks, and setting a few fires with the candles we had going. The problem was that the ceilings were too low to allow for enough drop for the paper to separate. Nobody got hurt, but they weren't happy either.

That New Year's Eve might have marked the turning point. Our time was running out, but we didn't know it. What little novelty there had been in our arrival had worn off. The locals didn't understand us, and they didn't want to understand us. After all the fucking, fighting, selling weed and blow on campus, robbing the place blind for food, and just being overall nuisances, the whole town was ready to get rid of us. But it wasn't drugs or sex or slapping around a few locals that got us in trouble—it was the fact that we couldn't find anywhere to eat past 10:00 p.m.

I couldn't stand how early these restaurants closed in town because it meant that when we were hungry at 2:00 a.m. we had nowhere to go and had to munch on whatever we had lying around. But we lived at a hotel, so we sat on a gold mine as far as food was concerned. The only problem was that they locked all that food behind a gate in the kitchen at night. It was a strong gate too, so there was no way we could jimmy it open, except that there was just enough room for us to shimmy inside. Once Lupo figured out how to get in, we raided the room every night. In hindsight, we were probably a bit flagrant.

For a while, they couldn't figure out why half the ice cream, chips, and the rest of the inventory was seriously depleted every morning.

They didn't have cameras then, so management couldn't understand how they were going through so much food. But it didn't take long for them to catch on. All it took was one of the local hillbilly cleaning people to rat us out after they emptied the trash. On top of that, they were so sick of our antics, and sick of picking up after us, that once the cleaning ladies, probably sisters, found our Mars Bars wrappers and open ice cream containers, they went right to the police and showed the evidence like we had pulled a heist.

Our last night in Maine, me and The Loop were sitting in the office talking. The cleaning crew had just left with a garbage bag full of stolen food wrappers, which didn't seem odd to us at all. But a few minutes later, we heard a loud bang on the door. We just looked at each other, wondering if this was some angry boyfriend out there looking for us, but it was worse. It was two local Maine police officers, and they're not known for their love of people from Massachusetts.

As soon as I opened the door, this big local cop said, "You two overstayed your welcome! Pack your fucking bags!" And he meant it too. They wanted us gone right then, and they weren't about to give us a moment to think. They even waited for us to get our shit together to go.

We were *persona non grata* in that town. When we finished packing, those cops actually escorted us to the edge of town, and the cop who had told us to pack our bags said, "You *wops* ever come back here, and you'll end up in a shallow grave in the hills!" I wanted to be offended and maybe shoot my mouth off a little, but I thought better of it under the circumstances.

So it was back to Boston for me, and I had just fucked up any chance of nailing down a decent job once I got home. This was bad.

I looked at myself in the rearview mirror with disgust as the gumballs flashed on top of the cruisers behind me. "Really, Joe? You can't even cut it in Waterville fucking Maine?"

Chapter 17:

DISCO DEEJAY OF THE YEAR

The Boston I returned to after my exile was unrecognizable and practically a lifetime away from what I remembered. A year hadn't passed since I'd left for Maine, and the original first-generation clubs were driven to extinction. I knew it had been changing—I had felt the shift, but I never imagined it would go so quickly. It wasn't until I got home that I could see it with fresh eyes. The metamorphosis was painfully obvious, and life as I knew it changed forever. The old clientele scattered, and the clubs rolled up.

Celebration killed Yesterday, and now Celebration was on its way to becoming a dive bar. Even the Rhino was closed. Zelda shut down immediately following a shooting. The whole building was boarded up and abandoned. It broke my heart every time I drove by. It was just like the end of the Copacabana in New York City—a landmark died. All the Zelda's people gathered after that and had a "Zelda Night" at another club. It was like an Irish wake, lots of tears and twice as much drinking.

At the same time the first-generation clubs were closing, Disco was commercially exploding and creeping into the oddest places. Every Chinese restaurant in Boston held a Disco after 10:00 p.m. *Saturday Night Fever* and John Travolta were a major catalyst. To top it off, venues that could hold a couple thousand people were now cropping up. John Addison, who was famous in New York for his Disco, *Le Jardin*, rented a huge space on Lansdowne Street, just three blocks away from the Kenmore and directly across from the Green Monster. He cleaned it up and opened a high-end club called *Boston Boston*. At the very same time, about a mile away in Copley Square, a bunch of investors got together and opened a swanky place called *Whimsy's* that held over a thousand people. Clubs like this brought the velvet rope to Boston, and the town was no longer a place to come party, listen to great music, make friends, and chase girls but a place to be seen. It was the dawning of the *poser*. And this is the point where the Rock 'n' Roll guys who had been knocked out by the rising Disco tide started building up their anti-Disco army.

On Christmas Eve 1978, WDAI cancelled local radio host Steve Dahl's rock show and switched formats to Disco. Dahl soon landed a morning show with WLUP and began mocking his former station's new slogan "Disco D.A.I.," calling it "Disco D.I.E." This got traction with his audience, and mocking Disco turned into a routine for him. He spoofed Rod Stewart's hit, "Da Ya Think I'm Sexy?" with his own, "Da Ya Think I'm Disco?" which actually got him onto the charts. He was really just mad that Disco forced him to get dressed and take a shower and learn to dance if he wanted to get a girl.

In the meantime, we had no idea that a backlash was forming against us or that Disco's poser side was all some people would ever know, which helped the "Disco Sucks" crowd even more.

One thing was apparent though: if that was how Zelda and the Rhino went out, then things were going to be even worse for me. But I fought the idea that I was a has-been and picked up small gigs to get back on my feet. I landed a lot of guest spots around town: gay clubs, black clubs, and weddings. But it wasn't the same, even though a great opportunity was about to fall into my lap.

One night in 1978, not long after my return from the Pine Tree State, I did a guest spot at Kimmy's in Kenmore Square, Cambridge, which sat right behind East Cambridge. It was at Kimmy's that I met up with Jack Donahue, an infamous bartender in Boston who I had known for some time. He was a total fucking character, the type of guy who could sell a harpoon to a whale. Everybody loved him. He was spinning bottles and juggling full glasses way before Tom Cruise ever did it in *Cocktail*. He was like a master hibachi chef, but with booze.

That night he pulled me off to the side. "I got something for you," he said.

I thought he meant blow, so naturally I held out my hand. "Okay, give it to me."

"No, you crazy fuck, it's something else."

"What?"

"I'm not gonna tell you. I'll show you tomorrow."

I drove myself crazy trying to figure out what he meant. Did he have a club for me? I started to get excited. For years he had told me how much he loved me as a deejay, so maybe he had something like that in mind.

He scooped me up at my place the next night and threw me into a limo with a bunch of gorillas. I was happy at first, but I was all *skeed* up and soon started getting paranoid. We all know how this goes: jump into a car with a bunch of guys you think are your friends, and suddenly it turns into a scene from *The Friends Of Eddie Coyle*, and I take a hit to the squash and get left in a saltmarsh on the North Shore for the crabs to eat. You never knew back then. You thought you knew somebody, and then they'd turn on you in a second. Boston was good for that. So one minute I was imagining I was on my way to a new adventure, and the next I was trying to figure out which gangsters I had pissed off. I had worked too many spots packed with wise-guys, and played too many angles, and now I was throwing a seven. It was all over.

I really should have laid off the blow because none of that happened. I thought we were going to head to Revere to look at a club, but the driver didn't take us over the Mystic River Bridge (which no longer exists). Instead, from the South End of Boston, he took a right and then another right onto Commonwealth Ave., and the first thing I thought was, "Zelda."

Sure enough, he pulled up in front of the old building. There was a ladder leaning against the wall. It looked like there was some renovating going on.

"No?" I yelped.

"Yeah, we got a new club here. The time has come for *Future*."

When he hit me with that line, I screamed like a little girl. I was so happy. He was opening a brand-new club, with a brand-new name—Future.

"What comes around goes around," he said with a grin across his face.

We got out of the car and walked to the front door. Jack tapped on it, and a Hispanic guy came out and greeted him with a hug.

He was one of the Columbian owners. Jack made the introductions, and we were given a brief tour. We looked around for a bit, as the place was almost done and they were just adding the finishing touches.

In two seconds, I went from feeling like it was all over to getting a gig in the spot where it all began for me. They had left almost nothing from the old place and had even knocked down some walls to open up more space, increasing capacity from 150 people to 350. Every thread of carpeting had been ripped up, and in its place were mirrored walls and parquet floors. The deejay booth sat up high, left of the dance floor, and they were even building a stage. The sound system was unbelievable, with JBL's everywhere. The only thing left from Zelda was the iconic Rockettes pastel mural, which was left as a kind of memorial to the old days. They kept Zelda's ashtrays though, but switched them to Future logos.

The Colombian owners had hired Jack Donahue as their front man. His job was to scout talent, and he in turn had grabbed me and a few of the old doormen from Zelda. One of the doormen was Burt, who was a great guy too. He was the kind of guy that would beat the piss out of you and then pick you up, apologize, and put you in a cab.

Jack even searched far and wide to find Babe, the greatest Boston waitress of all time, and made her the head waitress at Future. It was all coming together, straight out of my imagination.

Aside from scouting employees, Jack recruited clientele from other clubs. He had a pile of cash and party favors to go around town, and for weeks on end he went to every club in a stretch limo. He'd go into a club, buy five or six bottles of champagne, then sit back and wait. When the moment was right, he'd lean into the person next to him, the *right* person, and let them know in hushed tones that there was a new club opening in Zelda's old place. Then he'd share his champagne and insinuate how incredibly lucky they were to receive the intel.

"Shhhh. Don't tell anybody. I'm just letting you in on it," he'd say, knowing full well they would tell everybody and their mother. On top of that, he was dropping this spiel ten or twenty times a day. A week before the grand opening, he and I went on air with Ron Robin at WBOS to officially let the cat out of the bag. Everyone listened to his radio show. It was big news.

Opening night was unbelievable. As Frankie D. would say, it was, an "extravaganza."

Jack knew how to lay the groundwork for promoting the club, and we didn't even get any of the poser Disco crowd. It was the original cast, the devoted first-generation, like the old days. Everybody was dying to come back to a spot like this, but nobody could ever seem to make it work. The old crew was there and then some, with more money and new players.

I was getting paid $200 a night, which was a lot then, plus all the booze I could drink and all the coke I could snort. The booth was also designed in such a way that, as long as the door was locked, I could blow some lines and entertain girls. It was the treehouse of my dreams. The drugs seemed to have improved too. They didn't make me so nuts or stupid. To my credit though, I did tone it down a bit. I didn't drink as much, and we stopped the crazy benders that lasted three days straight.

The cops were under the assumption that this was a front for the cocaine business, which it was not. But this meant the police looked at the club as a target and were going to take these Colombians for every penny they could squeeze out of them. That being said, Boston's finest had to be careful of how they went about it. They couldn't act like pigs because guys with reps were there who were mobbed up. There was no doubt about it, though: this was a gangster club. Whitey Bulger moved in. And when Whitey walked into a room, the room whispered. He would send guys in to set him up near an exit, and you hardly ever saw him after that.

He came off like a decent guy. I'd even go so far as to call him a gentleman. But I didn't know who he was until his name was all over the papers. When the shit hit the fan about what he did and his relationship with the feds, everyone was surprised.

That wasn't our concern back then. We just put together a legendary club that somehow got all the right people together. Disco was bringing in hundreds of millions of dollars in revenue from all walks of life. It was "Disco-nomics," and everybody got trickled on. Disco made more money than any other musical genre then. In the short period from 1975 to 1979, you couldn't touch Disco. No other genre came close to the revenue that Disco brought in, and it was money not only for the record companies but for everybody. And the music, the good music before they watered us down, was strong.

Disco music was an escape from everyday life. There was a lot of miserable shit happening at the time, and the music was a way out, if only for a few short hours. It was like being on a deserted island, and after stumbling through the jungle for days, you pull open the palm leaves and see a party filled with all the right people.

Future was everybody's second chance. One thing we couldn't really recapture was the family feel, but it would probably be our last whirl on the merry-go-round anyway, and so we were going to make the most of it and ride this motherfucker 'til the wheels fell off.

Beyond the doors, in the real world, everything was changing. *Saturday Night Fever* hit us like an atomic bomb. At the time of its release, John Travolta was just coming off *Welcome Back Kotter,* where he played (you guessed it) a stupid grease ball. But in the new movie, he was depicted as the most intelligent guy in a crew of imbecile WOPs. It premiered in December '77 and was still packing theaters in August '78. As a result, Disco burned hotter than ever. But once that happened, everybody knew it was only a matter of time before the whole era went up in flames. I saw *Saturday Night Fever* the first week it came out and was bothered by the misrepresentation of Italian Americans as shallow and gaudy. The movie also illustrated something different than what we really were. It characterized the kind of Italians who never went across the bridge or through the tunnels to the city where the people were diverse. They never expanded their horizons or even wanted to. These guys worked the same jobs and went to the same clubs night after night. We laughed about it because these were the idiots that were supposed to represent us, but they acted more like bad coke and steroid guys from the fight clubs

out in the burbs. We couldn't relate to any character in the movie—
they were racist assholes, and suddenly we had that label too. People
who had never even set foot in a Disco felt the same way about us.
The movie had the same kind of negative impact *The Godfather* had
on Italians. After that movie came out, all Italians were gangsters.

The first generation had done all the heavy lifting. We desegregat-
ed the clubs in the midst of the most racially volatile time in Boston.
We created and drove a musical revolution that changed everything
from fashion all the way up to finance. For a moment, we had tak-
en over the world, and now we were reduced to a bunch of Tony
Maneros.

I did get a kick out of the movie, though, especially the dance
contests. The dancers in our clubs had better moves than anything
ever seen on television or in the movies. But all of a sudden, after
'78, we all took a step back and saw that the whole world was dancing like Tony Manero. It was blasphemous. The new generation was
shaped by the movies, and now these clowns were showing up to
the club every night and throwing out those Tony moves.

To make it even more profane, people were coming to the booth
requesting "John Travolta songs" from the soundtrack. As if he was
the artist.

"Listen, you stupid fuck! If you're gonna waste my time, the least
you should know is who fucking sang it, and it's not the actor from
the movie. Get away from my booth."

This movie was another boon for Rock 'n' Roll and those fucking
guys who couldn't dance and were mad about it. For a few years,
Rock had taken a backseat to Disco, but it was about to come out
of hiding in a big and ugly way. The punk and alternative movement
was also on the rise, and not far behind was a new British invasion,
powered by rhythmic, white pop artists.

Disco was officially cliché. It was time for me to reinvent myself; I just didn't know it yet.

That's when I won the award.

They held the awards that year at the Hilton Hotel in Manhattan. It was a big night, but I was dressed down. The Billboard Magazine Dance Music Awards, 1978. John Luongo had won Disco Deejay of the Year the year before. I was confident I would win this time around. Since Maine, and despite what was happening all around me, everything seemed to be coming up roses for me. The Brooklyn Dreams stood at the edge of the stage. They were a bunch of great goombahs, just coming off a couple of big records. The lead singer, Bruce Sudano, was married to Donna Summer. She was standing at the podium, ready to announce the winner.

"And the award for Disco Deejay of the Year for Boston, my hometown, is...Joey Carvello!" She had a big, beautiful smile on her face when she read that line. It was obvious she knew me—she knew most of the big deejays, especially the ones from Boston. She was beyond the queen of Disco at this point—she was a major popstar. No Donna, no Disco. And there she was, smiling at me. I could've just fuckin' died right there.

That award was the capstone of my time as a deejay. As I stood on the stage, happy that I had won, I also knew that it was over.

Despite what was coming for Disco, Ray Caviano, my all-time favorite promo guy, came to the afterparty that night, and began a whole new opportunity in the music for me. Ray and I were tight. We had a Promotion-Man/Deejay relationship that was top of the line.

At that point, the music and lifestyle were a legit phenomenon. Disco had gone from an underground gay, black, and Italian phenomenon to dictating what you heard on the radio and saw on TV. While the music was bigger, it wasn't exclusive to the clubs anymore either. As I explained, it would piss me off when people came up to my booth and asked for songs they'd heard on the radio before I even had a chance to play them—these were songs that radio broke outside the clubs. Before I went to Maine, Disco music was super-served almost exclusively to Disco deejays before it was served to Top 40 radio. Now the record labels were ramping it up and pushing new songs out to the public any way they could, and radio played a giant role. The clubs were no longer the touchstone in the way they had been before, and the radio guys were all in. They didn't give a shit; they just wanted to play the hits. To make things worse, Disco music was being mass-produced by people who had no business making Disco songs. In the clubs, we used to get ten bad and ten good songs a week; now we got ten good and twenty bad.

And this is where Ray came in. I already looked up to promo guys, but Ray Caviano was the man. I dug his style. He was unpretentious, aggressive in a positive way, and passionate—and he had great records. He was head of promotions for TK Records, which was arguably the first and most influential independent record label to produce music specifically for the clubs. Their roster was stacked with Disco artists who had massive club and radio hits, including KC and the Sunshine Band, Peter Brown, Voyage, and the Ritchie Family.

That night as Ray left the party, he turned and said, "We'll be talking, Joey."

What he had in mind I could never have guessed because he was about to get his own label under Warner Brothers, and he wanted me as his promotions guy for the East Coast.

Chapter 18:

DISCO DEMOLITION

Enter Steve Dahl—schlub that he was. Doing bits mocking Disco on his radio show became a profitable thing for him. After all, there were a lot of guys just like him who couldn't get girls and could never get it together enough to get into our clubs. There's a lot written out there painting Dahl as a homophobe or a racist, but I don't think that was it. Even though his "Do You Think I'm Disco?" is definitely focused on Italians in a bad way. At heart, Dahl's anger wasn't caused by racism or anything in that zone. He was just outside of a cultural movement that he couldn't take part in. It wasn't his style either—he didn't want to take a shower and wear clean clothes. And there were a lot of others who were just like him. Add to this the fact that the labels were pushing cliché and watered down music, and the clubs were packed with posers, and a lot of people turned off. This meant that Dahl's audience was growing, and when he was fired from WDAI Chicago because it switched formats to Disco, he developed a vendetta against the music that he brought to his new morning show at WLUP with a vengeance.

There, he became famous for chanting "Disco Sucks" and scratching Disco tracks over the airwaves. His routine culminated in the summer of 1979, when he organized Disco Demolition night with the ownership of the Chicago White Sox. It worked like this: if you brought in a Disco record for Dahl to destroy that night between games of a doubleheader, then you got into Comiskey Park for just ninety-eight cents. Bill Veeck, the owner of the team, was known for pulling these kinds of stunts. He was quoted that year saying something to the effect that even if they didn't have a winning team, the fans were still going to have fun. But the trouble with instigating thousands of people into having fun is that sometimes you get a riot, which is what they had on their hands that July night.

For starters, instead of pulling in something like 10,000 fans, the event drew in over 50,000 people, and these were people who didn't show up to watch a ball game. Truth be told, it was a decent PR stunt. Well, except for the fact that Chicago had to forfeit the second game of their doubleheader, and no one would work with their marketing director again.

Before the game, fans were told to drop their hated Disco records into a large crate which Dahl would later explode on the field. The story goes that so many fans brought records to the field that the box quickly filled and the remaining people had to take their records with them to the stands. At about that same time, management realized that more people had shown up for the game than the venue could hold and in turn locked the remaining crowds outside. These folks were unhappy, and security was then drawn away from the field to work the gates. It was a powder keg.

The place erupted once Dahl drove into the park in a Jeep dressed in a kind of army costume. The fans had started throwing anything that wasn't nailed down even before the maestro arrived. The hail of records, batteries, liquor bottles, and cherry bombs only grew worse once he made his long procession around the park and then out to center field driving the people into a frenzy. These crazy bastards, every one of them white and a lot of them motivated by racism, started throwing 45s like discuses onto the grass even when the players were still out. Some of the players reported that the records were sticking out of the ground like black gravestones before they got out of there. It was dangerous, and worse than that, the crowd was in an ugly mood and tuned up for a big show. Dahl took his time jazzing them up and then exploded the crate like Wile E. Coyote out in center field. The explosion was big enough to blow a hole in the turf that would prevent the next game from taking place. I don't know what they thought was going to happen. My guess is Dahl didn't care. He was there to make a point, and the worse things got, the better it was for him. At that point, nothing management did was going to stop the show. It had a life of its own.

As it turned out, blowing up the crate was not enough for the crew in the stands. They wanted more. A lot of the people still had records in hand and wanted to be part of the extravaganza. Within minutes, those fans stormed the field, where they made their own fire. At that point, they began throwing the old records they had actually brought with them onto the inferno. This was what they had come for, and it's the kind of success Dahl could only have hoped for. While the riot was bad for the team's ownership, it made Dahl a national figure overnight. Together with Dahl, the audience was there to trash an entire music category and the people that loved it; destruction was what they were out for.

The night had its effect. Within weeks, people were ashamed to admit they ever went to Discos, and acts that were on fire the year before couldn't get booked. Dahl, that prick bastard, took the air right out of our balloon and was happy about it.

This is more or less the way the story is typically told, but I think I should make a few observations. The fans didn't fill Dahl's crate with records they brought to the park that night. Instead, the record labels *themselves* filled the crates for Dahl. What the fans brought into

Comiskey they had to take into the stands, which is why they ended up with all those records to throw onto the field at the end.

I know for a fact that the labels had records drop-shipped to the park for that moment, probably to grease the skids in case the audience didn't provide enough props to make an impact.

I've talked with guys that shipped the records. If you don't believe me, just watch tape on the event—many of those records he blew up were still wrapped in their plastic wrap. How many people would purchase new records just to get into a ball game for ninety-eight-cents? Not many.

Now you're going to ask me, "why?" Why would the record labels drop ship the records to grease the skids for an event that would hurt their own cash cow?

My answer is that Disco hadn't just fallen out with a large segment of the population; it had lost favor with the labels themselves—both the higher-ups and the middle guys. The middle guys were turned off because when the bean counters had eventually realized how much money they were making off this music, they had forced the field staff to start promoting Disco, leaving a bad taste in their mouths and more. At that point, the VPs of promotion and local promoters grew to hate the music. They hated it even more because they were being forced to take it seriously when 90% of these guys were Rock 'n' Roll people. They couldn't relate to the Disco lifestyle; they thought it was gay, and they were all homophobic, and they looked like fish out of water trying to promote it and felt like sellouts whenever they did. This means that the guys the labels had out in the streets often hated what they were doing and had an interest in seeing it go away.

I knew how much they hated Disco because by January of '79 I had become RFC/Warner's head of promotion for the Northeast and Southeast. Ray Caviano really did come through. I won't go into those stories here but to say that I used to attend the weekly meetings in Woburn, Massachusetts for WEA, which was Warner, Elektra, and Atlantic, which also distributed RFC. I always got time to talk at these meetings, but no one ever listened to me. They didn't want to know about Disco. They thought the music was gay and everyone involved was a "fag," which they believed even more so of me because I was close to Sunny Joe White. And even though Sunny had built a huge audience at KISS 108 playing Disco, they didn't want to have to take him seriously either and were all just hoping they could get back to business as it had been.

That was how the mid-level guys felt about Disco, but the top-level guys had their feathers ruffled as well. Now, Disco as danceable music played in clubs was not going to die, and the labels had no intention of killing that either. But Disco as a cultural phenomenon was a problem for label heads because it was taking away their control to choose hits based on their own politics and bullshit. In other words, it was unacceptable that Joey Carvello from East Cambridge could break hits onto radio from a club in a Boston alley. The big boys at the labels wanted that sway. Also, if Donna Summer broke in the clubs, that meant the radio guys were playing catch up, and they didn't like that either. Most of the programmers wanted to be the ones to break these records first and didn't care if the labels spoon-fed them acts just as long as they maintained their chokepoint on the newest stuff.

I know exactly how this works also because after a short stint with Ray at RFC I worked promotion for Atlantic Records in the same offices. I wasn't happy with the two stiffs we had to promote that week, and so I was looking for a gem in the boxes of new singles we had on hand.

The two offenders were the Jim Carroll Band and their "People Who Died" and Fred Knoblock and "Why Not Me." Jim Carroll had just visited the branch the week before. Personally, I liked him. He was a decent guy and a successful author too. He wrote *The Basketball*

Diaries, which was a graphic account of his early teen years. It was published in 1978 and made into a movie starring Leonardo DiCaprio and Mark Wahlberg in 1995. But liking this guy didn't make his record any better. I was used to working records with titles and hooks like "I Wanna Be Your Lover" and "Dancer." Now all of a sudden, they expected me to get fired up about a song called "People Who Died." I didn't like the name. I liked the song even less.

Fred Knobloch was a singer/songwriter from Nashville. He was signed to the Scotti Brothers label, which we distributed. "Why Not Me" was a straight up twenty-five and over, female adult contemporary record. It made me want to open a vein. And the name Fred Knobloch ain't sexy either.

That being the case, I took it upon myself to spice things up a bit. Lo and behold, I came across a song on Cotillion Records, which was an "urban label" under the Atlantic umbrella. The song was by Stacy Lattisaw, "Let Me Be Your Angel." The moment I heard it, I thought it was a smash and decided to make that my priority for the week.

Major labels *face-valued* records without even listening to them: black artists to Urban Radio, white artists to Pop; everything in its category with different groups in control of each. And trust me when I tell you the majority of pop record reps were just fine with the urban artists staying in the urban zone and vice versa. It was the way it was then and hasn't changed much over the past forty years. But when I listen to a song, I listen for a hit. As soon as I heard "Let Me Be Your Angel," the promo man in me kicked in. I knew I had to get this song on radio, and fast. My first stop was KISS 108, dressed as an angel in a short skirt. There, Sunny Joe White was firmly ensconced as Boston's #1 deejay and media personality. Nobody had a more powerful or influential relationship with their listeners and peers than Sunny. He agreed to play the song. And that wasn't the only station I hit that day with great results. The song went over. And there was nothing like taking an obscure track by an unknown artist and blowing it the fuck up. I had a blast doing it too. What could be better?

That Friday, the branch secretary outside my office took a call for me.

"Joey, its Vince and Sam on line one."

This would be the brass calling to tell me I was the greatest promo guy in the world. I imagined the call would go something like this: "You took the initiative to go out and get a record you believed in played. Great job!"

Instead it went like this:

Vince Faraci, Senior VP of Promotion out of the New York office of Atlantic, started by saying, "Joey, you motherfucker!! Who the fuck do you think you are? Who the fuck told you to go out there and promote that fucking record?"

"What are you talking about, Vince? I worked the others too. I got the Jim Carroll Band on at BCN. I couldn't do anything with Knoblock, but I will next week."

"You don't set the priorities! I set the priorities! If you want to get records played that you like, then you should get into radio! You're fucking fired! Pack your shit and get the fuck out!"

That was that. I broke Stacy Lattisaw as a multi-platinum recording artist and got fired for it, so I know from real life just how important controlling hits is to record labels. And Disco—not just in Boston, but in every city south to Miami and east to Detroit—was making its own bones at that time. Some club only a few thousand people knew about could turn a local track into a regional hit that could go nationwide. This was not the order of things labels wanted, and it had to be stopped and it had to be reorganized.

On another level, the small black—that is, African-American—labels were losing their acts to mainstream labels because their artists were crossing over in the clubs to popular (or white) audiences. It doesn't matter that we were talking about a smaller piece of the pie; that piece was their piece, and they didn't like the disruption.

Those were the interests that didn't want Disco to continue in the way it had been going. Couple this with a backlash in the street from the Rock 'n' Roll rank and file and you get a recipe for what happened in Comiskey Park. The labels were interested in letting the air out of the Disco balloon and transitioning to something they could better control that wasn't a threat. That's why within weeks of Disco Demolition Night, guys like Nile Rodgers couldn't get a call back. That's why record labels immediately killed their Disco departments; it's also why 1980 was the first and last year the Grammys had a Disco category. It didn't happen by accident. One asshole in Chicago didn't have that much pull. The labels pulled for him. They wanted Disco as a cultural force dead, and when they saw an opportunity to give it a push, the power did all it could to knock it over.

Steve Dahl didn't kill Disco by himself—the record labels helped him do it.

As to the other knock on him, I know he takes a lot shit because people say Disco Demolition night was all racist and homophobic, but that's not how it went down. Of course racists and homophobes were there, but it was mainly a reaction to mainstream Disco. First and foremost, the guys at Comiskey Park hated *Saturday Night Fever* and the Bee Gees. They rolled their eyes at the general-purpose Discos in Chinese restaurants and loathed the fake Tony Maneros of the world, and that was all straight stuff. In a way, the image these guys were reacting to was sick and dying.

So the reason Steve Dahl should take shit isn't for racism or anything else—it's because he was a tool the interested parties used to move on to something less threatening, and he hurt a lot of people with that stunt.

CODA

I was cleaning up the backstop in Thorndike Park, East Cambridge, when a black Lincoln started circling the perimeter. It was another patronage gig I had acquired when I got back from Alabama and the Army, and so I was biding my time. But I had never seen that car before. Then it jumped the curb and raced across the field toward me. I ran, but there was a fence blocking the way and before I knew it the car was right behind me. If the right guys had been in that car, I wouldn't have gotten a second chance. As it stood, the car ground to a stop, the door swung open hard enough to bounce back off the hinges, and a monster appeared over the frame—a yeti in a slept-in suit with a shitload of white hair.

I took a breath when I recognized him. "Oh. Hi, Tip," I said.

"Tip? Tip? You son of a bitch bastard! You call me Congressman O'Neill! You know who I am!" he shouted.

Tip O'Neill was a scary guy. He was also a legend in Boston politics who had worked himself up through the ranks to become a United States Congressman and was soon-to-be Speaker of the United States House of Representatives who would famously work with Ronald Reagan. But at this point, he was still a local junkyard dog. He was six-foot-five, 280 pounds, and the earth shook when he approached me. I could feel his steps by home plate.

"If it weren't for that call from your Uncle Frankie, you'd be in a hole in Leavenworth," he said, getting closer.

"Damn," I thought, "Uncle Frankie *does* know everyone."

"I got you out," he went on with his finger in my face, "and it caused me and your family a lot of fucking embarrassment too! That garbage you pulled down south put me in a difficult position."

I had nothing to say. But he wasn't waiting for a response, he was there to let me know, "If you fuck up like that again, I'm going to put you in a barrel myself! I got the okay from your old man too."

And that was that. He spun on his heel in the first base line, climbed back into the Lincoln, and his driver pulled off the diamond in a cloud of dust. Patronage gigs had their perks and their price. The price was guys like him knew where they could find you.

I never knew how I got out of Leavenworth until that moment. All I was told was that Uncle Frankie had pulled some strings because, as usual, he knew the guy. I just didn't know the guy was the future Speaker of the United States House of Representatives.

I know now that if they hadn't pulled those strings for me all those years ago, I'd be writing an entirely different book about life in jail and East Cambridge gangs; or I'd be dead. Instead, I had the music. And as much as Congressman O'Neill and Uncle Frankie got me out of a long bid in Leavenworth, it was the music that saved me from the streets—saved me from myself.

I know the music did the same for a lot of people. And more than just bringing us up, it brought us all together. All those dreams of the civil rights generation were largely realized out on those sweaty dance floors and those late nights, at least on the East Coast—out in L.A., Disco never went over.

Those changes were something I was part of. I grew up in the Boston ghettos. Mine was just an Italian one. Even though they had hearts of gold, aside from political interests, most of my relatives didn't want to accept the Irish in their neighborhoods, let alone into their families. I'm not just picking on Italians either—the Irish were the same way, and so were the Poles, and if you think black people didn't largely have an identical attitude, then I know you didn't live anywhere near one of those ethnic neighborhoods. With our roots in those places and families and in that kind of thinking, everybody then was practically destined to remain stuck inside the same ruts, destined to stay on the same corners. But the thing that shook us all up was the Discotheque. And for a little while, if you could make it in the club, it didn't matter what neighborhood you were from. But "making it" meant more than just dancing. And it was so much more than strunz's like Tony Manero stuck in his neighborhood could ever have offered us. Disco never could have existed if the Tony Maneros built it or even if it was like the Studio 54 scene where the stars were out looking at each other. In that respect and compared to those later New York clubs, what we had was like the Paradise Garage, where stars or not, Grace Jones and Mick Jagger or not, they were just a bunch of sweaty kids on the floor getting crazy. The truth is that people from every hood and burg built another culture together inside the Discotheques.

I know it didn't hold together, but there was a brief moment, at about the time when the Village People played in Celebration, when many clubs were as close to fully integrated as they ever would be. Almost nothing like that had ever existed, and the soft (sometimes hard) segregation of clubs seemed like a thing of the past.

The truth is that, aside from a boycott here and there, we didn't need force to open up the clubs. In my case, the people wanted it that way—that's why so many of my friends walked out at Yesterday when management wanted to toss the Peña brothers. We all understood each other, and anyone who came in, anyone who was happy in the atmosphere, was our friend, and our friends were family. I think that's the only point. We were treating each other with love and respect because that's what people wanted. A couple of guys needed to get taken out the back door and thrown into a dumpster every once in a while to facilitate what we had, but that just made it safer for everybody. At one point, Gypsies were silently watching out so that a mixed audience didn't get robbed by predatory thieves. I think that was Disco as much anything else we remember. And I think that combination was too scary for the major players to let happen. The godfathers of the record industry, black, white and everything else, saw their interests jeopardized by mixed audiences who found out that they could have as much or more in common with people from a different neighborhood when they had similar interests. And that combination started breaking hits. In turn, the money felt like it had given up too much and wanted to get back as much control of music on the street level as they could, and so they divided it and conquered it and then rebranded it as the dance music we got in the early eighties. The only difference was that there was firmer corporate control over who could make hits. That, more than anything, is the way the story of Disco should be told. I think that way because I lived through it.

1977, Brothers 4, Nashua, New Hampshire. 1st Generation Boston
Deejays, left to right: "Captain Wendell" Edmonds, Calvin "Cosmo" Wyatt,
Joey Carvello, Danae Jacovidis, In the booth, Steven Burke.

TOP 6

1. DREAMIN A DREAM ... CROWN HEIGHTS AFFAIR
2. DO IT ANYWAY YOU WANT ... PEOPLES CHOICE
3. GET DOWN TONIGHT ... K.C. & SUNSHINE BAND
4. BRAZIL ... RITCHIE FAMILY
5. WHAT A DIFFERENCE A DAY MAKES ... ESTHER PHILLIPS
6. I COULD HAVE DANCED ALL NIGHT ... ARCHIE BELL

EXTRAS

PARTY MUSIC ... PATTI LUND (Joe Carvello - Yesterday)
LADY LADY LADY ... BOO IE MAN ORCHESTRA (Joe - Yesterday)
Get Off Your Ass ... Funkadelic (John T.C. Luongo - Rhinoceros)
One Way Street ... Becket Brown (Danae - Styx)
When You're Young & In Love ... Ralph Carter (Tom Moulton -
                                        as part of N.Y.C.'s Top 3)
Peace Pipe ... B.T. Express (Tom Moulton - Disco Action/Billboard)
Hooked on Life ... Trammps

FEATURE

Interview with Bimbo Jet who have members from Puerto Rico,
Dominican Republic, Spain, France, Italy, & Panama. A very
exciting act.

El Bimbo (only) was played. I do not have album.

DISCO NOTES

Details next week from Joe Carvello & John Luongo about a
$4,000 dance contest at Yesterday & about the Ultra Disco
both coming up in September.

A mention that Ron Robin has a regular "Disco Notes" feature
in NightFall Magazine.

Some of the music on Disco Notes is supplied by Everett Music
just off Everett Square ... You guessed it ... In Everett.

See Ya

Ron Robin

RON ROBIN'S "DISCO NOTES".

1975, Yesterday's $1,000 Dance Contest contestants, including Deejays: third from left, Donnie Goff; middle, MC Joey Carvello; peeking out, Brian Harkins; Lower Right, "Ruffy" Mugica.

The Winners! "Ruffy" and Anne.

Shelly and Joey Carvello, Yesterday's Boat Cruise, 1975.

JOEY, BELLA, AND JOHNNY GIACHETTO.

JULY, 1970 IN CONNIE'S KITCHEN ON
THORNDIKE STREET, EAST CAMBRIDGE;
LEFT TO RIGHT: JOE PACELLI, RICHARD
"CAPPY" CAPOBIANCO, RAY GERANEO, BILLY
BARASSO, RICHARD "RICKY" MACIEJKO.

1977, LEFT TO RIGHT: RON ROBIN, JOHN "TC" LUONGO, SALSOUL RECORDING
ARTIST GARY CRISS, JOEY, "DISCO VINNIE" PERUZZI.

1977, Celebration/Kenmore Club.

1977, Celebration/Kenmore Club
Joey with "Wolfman Jack".

1979, Joey with Prince at The
Paradise, Comm. Ave. Boston.

1978, JOEY WITH JACK DONAHUE AT FUTURE/CACHÉ.

PRESENTED TO

JOE CARVELLO

DISCO DEEJAY OF THE YEAR

Boston

June 1978

Billboard

YESTERDAY
cordially invites you to the

First Anniversary Party for
DISCO JOE CARVELLO
"A star on the disco scene"

Hors d'oeuvres — Champagne

MONDAY
AUGUST 11, 1975
at 7:00 p.m.

YESTERDAY
Kenmore Square
Boston

Warner Bros. Records

invites you to the dawn

of the 80's.......

RFC Records...........

a Disco Celebration.

Time: 9 pm

Place: Studio 54

Date: February 5th 1979

PHOTO PAGES COURTESY OF MICHELLE HIRSCH, CARIL MITRO, LINDA SCURINI, RICKY MACIEJKO.

Cecil B's Discothéque

ALLOW US TO INTRODUCE OURSELVES! WE ARE MAINE'S ALL NEW TOTALLY SOPHISTICATED DISCOTHEQUE. OUR NAME IS CECIL B'S.

FOR YEARS MAINE HAS LOOKED FOR A TRULY TOTAL DISCOTHEQUE. LOOK NO FURTHER - CECIL B'S IS LOCATED AT THE HOWARD JOHNSON'S MAINE FENWAY HOTEL ON MAIN ST., WATERVILLE.

BY COMBINING AN ELABORATE DECOR, SOPHISTICATED LIGHT SHOW, AN INCREDIBLE SOUND SYSTEM, COMFORTABLE ATMOSPHERE AND UNIQUE SPECIAL EVENTS AND PARTIES, WE ARE PRESENTING A DISCOTHEQUE FOR THOSE WHO SEEK THE FINER THINGS IN LIFE.

AS AN ADDED ATTRACTION CECIL B'S HAS ACQUIRED ONE OF THE COUNTRIES LEADING DISCO DISC JOCKEYS AND PERSONALITIES RIGHT FROM BOSTON, MASS. AND HIS NAME IS JOEY CARVELLO, AND HIS REPUTATION STRETCHES TO L. A. HE IS KNOWN AS THE "MAESTRO OF THE DISCO MIX". NOT ONLY WILL YOU HEAR THE POPULAR DISCO MUSIC OF TODAY BUT ALSO THE DISCO HITS OF TOMORROW.

SO- TOMORROW IS TODAY - AT CECIL B'S DISCOTHEQUE.

Re~Grand Opening

Thursday   October 13, 1977

8 pm ~ 1 am   free champagne

WATERVILLE, MAINE.

"Hope you had a nice day!" from The Boston Record Pool on
Comm. Ave. in Kenmore Square at rush hour.